# SOUTHWARK PAST

First published 2001 by Historical Publications Ltd
32 Ellington Street, London N7 8PL
(Tel: 020 7607 1628  Fax: 020 7609 6451)

**ISBN 0 948667 72 9**
British Library Cataloguing-in-Data
A catalogue record for this book is available from the British Library

Typeset in Palatino by Historical Publications
Reproduction by G & J Graphics, EC2
Printed by Edelvives in Zaragoza Spain

# THE ILLUSTRATIONS

*The following kindly gave their permission for illustrations to be reproduced:*

Peter Jackson Collection: *11, 105*
London Metropolitan Archives: *98, 102*
J. Sainsbury plc: *106*
Slade School Archive: *114*
London Borough of Southwark: *47, 49, 139, 141, 146 and the jacket illustration*

Illustration 135 was taken from *London's Fire Brigades* by W. Eric Jackson (1966), source,
despite investigation, unknown.
All other illustrations were supplied by the publisher.

# SOUTHWARK PAST

## Richard Tames

HISTORICAL PUBLICATIONS

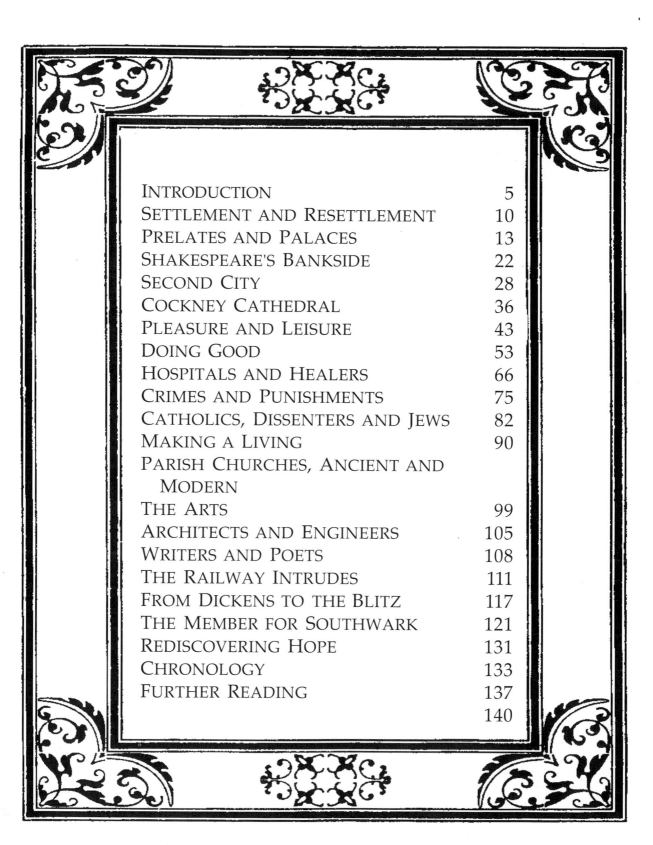

# Introduction

Professor Nikolaus Pevsner once asserted that "Southwark is more intimately London than any other borough". Ian Nairn offered a similar observation in slightly more mischievous terms – "London is bent around the Thames; however much the north bank might wish to forget it, the south holds the centre of gravity." Symbolic of both that centrality and the paradoxes of its location stands Southwark Cathedral, the largest ancient building south of the river, yet overshadowed by modern tower-blocks and hemmed in by Victorian railway arches and market buildings. Within can be found both a memorial to Shakespeare and a chapel dedicated to sufferers from AIDS. To quote the elegant words of the official guide: "Its monuments speak of a rich past, its altars of an inexhaustible grace".

In an evocative essay on Istanbul Jan Morris characterises that most ancient city as built upon layer on layer of history, stamped as it were into the earth. Southwark can match it for two millennia, at least. In the Cuming Museum is part of a standard once borne by a Roman legionary. Where Tate Modern stands were once a wharf called Moulstrand and ponds where pike were kept for the days when monks were forbidden meat. Later the site accommodated the Phoenix gas works and the London Hydraulic Power Company and, from 1891, an electric power station which drove the newspaper presses of Fleet Street across the river. In the shadow of Giles Gilbert Scott's monumental power station lies Hopton Street, once Green Walk, where eighteenth-century almshouses and a detached house from c.1702 still stand. Around its northern end once stood the Swan theatre, the celebrated Falcon Inn, Epps Cocoa factory and a glassworks renowned for the quality of both its ornamental and utilitarian output. Mint Street Adventure Playground occupies the site of a former workhouse. The triangular site north of St Saviour's war memorial is now largely given over to serving food and drink in various forms but in Victorian times it accommodated a bank and an insurance office, before that the town hall, before that a debtors' prison, before that a medieval parish church. Union Street is only a little over two centuries old as a thoroughfare and although it cannot boast a pedigree to compare with, say,

Tooley Street, it is packed with the past nonetheless. It once contained a paupers' burial ground, a workhouse, a Congregational church, a music hall, a hop warehouse, a parish school, Sainsbury's bacon-curing stoves and the business premises of Hayward Brothers 'Architectural Ironmongers', Ashby's tea and coffee packers, James Adams, inventor of the pneumatic door hinge and the manufacturers of the laudanum-based Dr J. Collis Browne's Chlorodyne. Local architect George Gwilt lived there in a house he had himself designed and in June 1944 a V1 exploded there in the borough's most lethal single bombing incident, killing more than fifty.

As in so many other parts of London, Southwark's history and heritage are recalled in the names of its alleys, streets and thoroughfares. The most common refer to local property owners, such as Montague, Ewer, Newcomen, Lant, Hopton, Thrale and West. Ufford is the family name of the first earl of Suffolk. Sinister

*1. Southwark is forever associated with the Tabard inn at which Geoffrey Chaucer (1340-1400) had his pilgrims assemble for their journey in Canterbury Tales. This oil of Chaucer is by an unknown artist.*

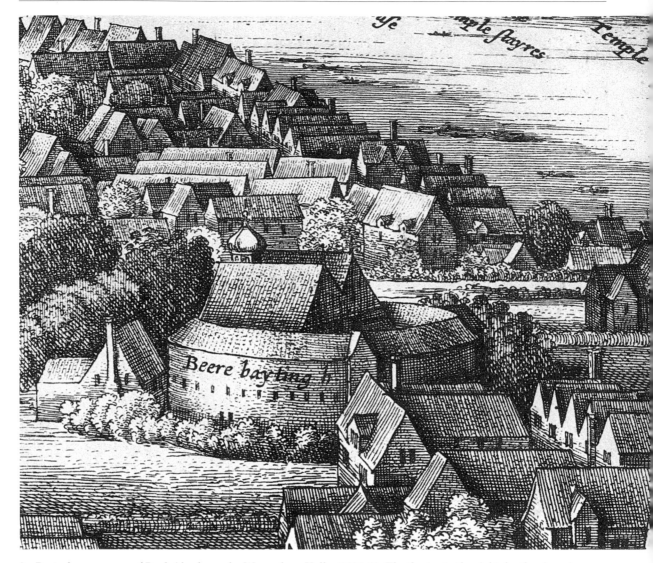

2.  *Part of a panorama of Bankside, drawn by Wenceslaus Hollar 1636-42. The theatre to the right, by the river, is incorrectly named The Globe. In fact, it is The Hope.*

Deadman's Place, now no more, may have been merely a corruption of Desmond. Paris Garden harks back to Robert de Paris of the reign of Richard II, though the area was also subsequently to be referred to confusingly as Palace Garden and 'the Parish Garden'.

The palatial residences of the proud prelates of medieval times survive in the names of Winchester Walk and Rochester Walk. Bankside, Broadwall and Upper Ground derive from the age-long battle to hold back the tidal Thames. Many other lost landmarks are similarly recalled – Bear Gardens for the bear-baiting ground, Park Street from the spacious grounds of Winchester House, Clink Street from its associated prisons, Marshalsea Road from the royal gaol so designated, Mint Street and Sanctuary Street from the local coining-house which later gave its name to a refuge for criminals and vagabonds. Other aspects of Southwark's disreputable past have been obscured by the renaming of Theeves Lane as St Thomas Street and Dirty Lane as Great Suffolk Street. Rose Alley comes from the Rose theatre, Bowling Green Place and Tennis Street from recreations favoured by loosely-imprisoned debtors to while away their days. Union Street was the site of the workhouse which served the local 'union' of parishes. Crooked Bandyleg Walk has disappeared, as have Barge House Steps where the royal barges were housed in Tudor and Stuart times. Porter Street takes its name from the heavy ale which was once a speciality of the local breweries and much favoured by the porters of the area's markets as a means of "putting the sweat back in". Mermaid Court, White Hart Yard and Falcon Point embody the names of famous former inns. Sawyer Street and Glasshill Street recall just two of the dozens of crafts once associated with the locality.

Geoffrey Chaucer's local connections are clearly hallowed in Pilgrimage Street and Tabard Street, named for the inn from which his Canterbury pilgrims famously departed, and less obviously in Talbot Yard and Manciple Street. The name of the former, denoting a hunting dog now more familiar as a Dalmatian, replaced Tabard when that inn was rebuilt, and the latter refers to one of the pilgrims, a sort of medieval monastic catering manager. The other local literary giant, Charles Dickens is acknowledged in Copperfield Street, Pickwick Street, Weller Street and Little Dorrit Court.

3 & 4.  Above, a depiction of the Tabard inn off Borough High Street, probably representing its appearance before the disastrous Southwark fire of 1676. By then it was usually known as the Talbot, shown below in c1829. A tabard was a sleeveless jacket and a talbot a species of hunting dog. The inn was demolished c1873 and Talbot Yard marks its site.

5. *The Canterbury Pilgrims as depicted in 1807 by Thomas Stothard (1755-1834), librarian of the Royal Academy.*

Other celebrities thus esteemed are no less real for being of more local import. Ayres Street honours a humble heroine. When fire broke out in an oil-merchant's premises in Union Street one day in 1885 nursemaid Alice Ayres passed three children to safety but was too late to save herself and died from her injuries after falling from the blazing building. Keyworth Street memorializes Leonard Keyworth, a Lincolnshire man who fought with a local South London battalion to win the Victoria Cross in 1915. Treveris Street honours a Flemish printer, Lockyer Street a prosperous pill-pusher, Dolben Street a fighting bishop and Crosby Row a pugnacious Lord Mayor. Rennie Street is for a doyen among engineers, Lancaster Street for a pedagogical pioneer, Sumner Street for a financially astute bishop who funded local schools, Meymott Street for a local administrator and antiquary and Thomas Doyle Street for the progenitor of St George's Catholic Cathedral.

Archaeology has revealed that the history of the Borough and Bankside stretches back to Neolithic times. Since the Romans that history has been a roller-coaster ride of alternating periods of expansion and contraction, prosperity and impoverishment. For centuries London's gateway, this part of the present borough of Southwark has variously been renowned for prelates, printing, prisons, prostitution and provisioning. Long a centre for learning and dealing and healing, over the last quarter century the area has reinvented itself yet again to become a centre of entertainment and enjoyment as it was in Shakespeare's day. The roller-coaster is once more definitely on the up.

# Settlement and Resettlement

## BEGINNINGS

Two thousand years ago the Thames shoreline at Southwark, now firmly embanked and crammed with large buildings, was a miniature archipelago of small, sandy islands, criss-crossed with channels and streams. The marshy nature of this area was to encourage ribbon development southward, along ridges of higher or firmer ground, with the intervening channels being used as ditches for drainage or transport and sometimes as boundary markers between properties.

Human activity on Bankside dates back some six millennia. The discovery of an antler mattock where Tate Modern now stands implies that the light soils of the shoreline islands, and perhaps their easy access to fresh water and fishing, attracted prehistoric settlement, at least on a temporary or occasional basis. Flint scrapers and knife blades and the postholes of circular huts have been found at Hopton Street and on the site of Guy's Hospital. A complete bowl was also found to have been deliberately buried in a small pit at Hopton Street, possibly as an offering to now unknown divinities. Neolithic pottery, decorated with impressions made by bird bones and twisted cord has been uncovered in St Thomas's Street, where there was an Iron Age farmstead. Pottery, pits and postholes confirm that there was another where Tooley Street now runs. At London Bridge there was a Bronze Age barrow, containing the cremated remains of at least five people, four of them children.

## THE ROMANS

Finds of Roman pottery, tesserae and fragments of painted wall plaster have been dated to the very earliest stages of the Roman occupation, between the Claudian invasion of AD43 and the Boudiccan revolt of AD60-61. Indeed, so many coins of the emperor Claudius have been recovered locally that it has even been suggested that during the first decade of London's development the major focus of activity may have been at the Southwark, rather than at the City end of the bridge. This may not seem unreasonable, given that the occupiers would have been as intent on securing the hinterland between the bridge and the coasts which linked them to their continental bases as they may have been on pushing further into the hostile interior.

The construction of London Bridge is normally conjectured at around AD50. Even as a wooden structure it represented a considerable engineering achievement, for it stood on stone piles and the river, though much more shallow, was then at least twice as wide as it is today. Roman Southwark developed between the southern end of the bridge and the point of convergence of two major long-distance routes, Stane Street, which ran south-west to Chichester, and Watling Street, which ran south-east to the Kentish coast. Within a decade Southwark was important enough for Boudicca's rebels to cross the river and burn it, a catastrophe from which the infant suburb appears to have swiftly recovered.

By AD100 the refounded Roman settlement stretched from about a third of a mile along the river frontage and half a mile inland to the south. Extending over such an area would have made it about one-seventh of the size of Londinium itself on the northern bank of the Thames. What is now Borough High Street, as the then approach road to the wooden Roman bridge, was lined with buildings, initially of timber and clay, later of stone. There may also have been an imposing colonnade or arcade flanking it at the bridge approach, where the Jubilee Line ticket hall now stands. Archaeological evidence suggests the premises of a baker, a butcher and a blacksmith, as might be expected on a busy thoroughfare. There were also local craftsmen working in bronze, leather and antler bone. Fragments of armour and horse-fittings imply a military presence, perhaps a picket routinely scanning travellers entering or leaving Londinium via the bridge. The shoreline itself was stabilised by wood revetments which were much sturdier than their Anglo-Saxon replacements. Nearby stood long, low warehouses, some sunk into the ground and consequently damp and cool, ideal for storing large amphorae of the imported dietary essentials unavailable locally, such as olive oil, wine, figs and liquamen, the fermented fish sauce used to flavour so many Roman dishes. Southwark finds of imported goods include a novelty lamp in the shape of a foot, from Holland, pottery from Gaul and Cologne and fish sauce from Antibes. Set among the warehouses may have been comfortable dwellings appropriate to prosperous merchants. A Roman building in Clink Street had a hypocaust, affording residents the luxury of

6. *The remains of a Roman round-bottomed, ocean going boat, found during construction of nearby County Hall in 1910. It is now in the Museum of London.*

under-floor heating in at least five rooms. Painted walls, tessellated floors and glazed windows are other indicators of a comfortable lifestyle. In 1977 a Roman well and sculptures, including one of a hunter-god, were found beneath the crypt of Southwark Cathedral. Analysis of middens confirms that the local diet was certainly varied and rich in fish and fruit. A third century timber tank beside a former watercourse near Guy's Hospital may have been used to hold oysters or fresh fish before they were sold on to consumers. The discovery in 1958 of the remains of a Roman boat on the site of Guy's shows that some, at least, of these watercourses were broad enough to be navigable.

Roman Southwark at its greatest extent may have covered twenty to twenty-four hectares.

The clear abandonment of three sites in the second century, coupled with a layer of earth revealing the conversion of formerly residential locations to gardens, implies a substantial loss of population from that time onwards. This would parallel a general decline in the population of Londinium as a whole. The contraction of the settlement is further confirmed by burials on the site of former buildings, the Romans being sticklers for respecting hygiene regulations which stipulated that burials must always be located outside settlements. Occupation appears, however, to have continued until the late fourth century, when iron and pottery objects were still being made locally. An almost total lack of archaeological finds for the period 400-850 suggests virtually complete desertion, quite possibly precipitated by the total decay of the bridge.

## RENEWAL

Recurrent Viking attacks in the London area from 842 onwards open a new chapter in Southwark's history. The first written reference to Southwark occurs in a document known as the *Burghal Hideage*, a survey of lands designated for the support of fortified places. Historians have traditionally dated this to *c*.914 but in 1982 the distinguished medievalist R H C Davis suggested that it might date from 886, i.e. when Alfred of Wessex ordered his son-in-law Edmund to reoccupy London and refortify its walls. Whatever the date of the document, description of a 'Suthringa geweorche' ("a defensive work of the men of Surrey") implies some kind of fortified bridgehead, an impression confirmed by the later *Olaf Saga* which describes 'Suthvirki' as "a great trading place", defended by "large ditches", which archaeology confirms to have been four metres across. The bridge itself might very possibly have been reconstructed on the original Roman piers. By the tenth century Southwark may have recovered sufficiently to have had a minster and a mint. There is evidence of quayside construction but of flimsy quality compared to Roman work.

In 1012 London fell to the Danish Sweyn Forkbeard. In 1014 Olaf of Norway joined forces with Aethelred II ('the Unready' – i.e. 'lacking in Counsel') to help that ill-favoured ruler regain the city. The *Olaf Saga*, an Icelandic composition of the thirteenth century by Snorre Sturlason, tells how Olaf's men tore down houses in Southwark to build wooden screens over their boats as protection against missiles. Fastening hawsers to the piles of London Bridge they hauled against them, aided by the ebbing tide, until they brought the superstructure crashing down, to the destruction of the Danes. The author of the *Saga* invokes the intervention of pagan divinity to explain Olaf's feat:

> London Bridge is broken down,
> Gold is won and bright renown,
> Shields resounding,
> War horns sounding.
> Hildur shouting in the din;
> Arrows singing
> Mailcoats ringing
> Odin makes our Olaf win!

Sturlason thus pointedly ignores the fact that Olaf had actually been baptised recently and subsequently took Saxon priests back with him to Norway to spread the gospel. Much good that did him as this missionising provoked a national revolt in which Olaf himself was slain in 1030. Death at the hands of pagan rebels at least secured the martyred monarch the posthumous comfort of canonisation. In Southwark, anglicized as Olave, Olaf was to be commemorated in the dedication of a parish church, first mentioned in 1096, which stood at the very foot of the bridge he once so famously destroyed. Art Deco St Olaf house now occupies the site, its façade carrying a portrait of the saintly warrior in the style of a medieval church wall-painting. Tooley Street itself derives from a severed corruption of the battling king's sainted name – by 1506 it was known as 'Seynt olyffes strete'.

The *Anglo-Saxon Chronicle* fails to record the colourful episode of breaking the bridge but does allege that in 1016 another Danish king, Knut, successfully recaptured London by digging a ditch to the south of Southwark so that his vessels could by-pass it and threaten the City from the west by sailing up the river Fleet. The scale of such an operation may seem improbable but the pre-existence of substantial drainage ditches which might only need enlargement or dredging implies that it would not be impossible.

Having survived the depredations of Sweyn and Olaf, Southwark became the scene of an inconclusive stand-off between the forces of Earl Godwin and Edward the Confessor in 1051. No substantial damage seems to have occurred then but at the time of the Norman conquest Southwark was put to the torch by a raiding-party of five hundred of the invaders in retaliation for an attempted sortie by London's militia.

Recovery appears to have been rapid because by the time of the Domesday survey, twenty years later, Southwark is recorded as having a dock, a herring fishery and no less than fifty houses in the possession of eleven manorial landholders in Surrey. These dwellings may have had a number of uses – to act as a depot for the sale and distribution of estate produce to Londoners, as a *pied-a-terre* during visits from the country on business and in some cases perhaps to yield a rental income as well. This reflects a common later practice by absentee landlords, leasing off a property for occupation while reserving the right of occasional accommodation and hospitality when needed.

# Prelates and Palaces

## MANORS AND PARISHES
Medieval Southwark consisted of five autonomous manors. The smallest, covering the immediate area either side of the southern end of London Bridge and known from the fourteenth century as the Guildable manor, belonged to the Crown. Stretching south and east of this in an irregular arc was the Archbishop of Canterbury's manor, known from the sixteenth century as the Great Liberty. To the west of the Guildable manor was the manor of the Bishop of Winchester, known by the sixteenth century as the 'liberty of the Clink'. The manor to the west of that, held first by Cluniac monks, then the Templars until their dissolution under Edward II and then by the Hospitallers until 1536, was initially known as 'the Wilys' (i.e. Willows) and from the fourteenth century as 'Paris Garden'. To the south of the Clink and Paris Garden was the largest manor,

*7. Part of a plan of Southwark, dated 1540*

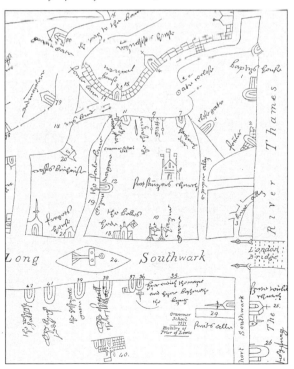

roughly equal in size to both of them added together. Originally held by the prior of Bermondsey, from the Reformation onwards this became known as the King's or Queen's manor.

The five manors were paralleled by five parishes, whose boundaries coincided only partly with them. The smallest, St Mary Magdalene, covering the westernmost third of the Guildable manor, was a tiny enclave around what is now Southwark Cathedral (then St Mary's Priory), catering for its lay residents. South of that and about twice as large, was St Thomas's focused on the Hospital, dedicated to the twelfth-century martyr, Thomas à Becket. St Olave's lay to the east, roughly corresponding to the northern half of the Great Liberty. To the west St Margaret's accounted for both the Clink and Paris Garden. St George's represented most of the King's Manor.

## ERA OF EXPANSION
For Southwark the two and a half centuries after the Norman conquest were a period of continuing expansion and prosperity, terminated by a major national famine of 1315-16, which was occasioned by a complex environmental catastrophe involving floods, cattle plague and failed harvests. The population of early medieval Southwark may have expanded about ten-fold, from around five hundred to about five thousand, elevating the community from one-fiftieth the size of London to one-twentieth. Already by the thirteenth century the documented evidence of personal names suggests incomers attracted from Scotland, Ireland, France, Germany, Lombardy, Norway and the Low Countries. In 1295 Southwark was accorded the dignity of a parliamentary borough, being represented in Edward I's 'Model Parliament' despite the fact that its administrative status was, strictly speaking, confused and anomalous. The probable pre-Conquest minster (and present Cathedral) was reorganised around 1106 as an Augustinian priory dedicated to St Mary. St Thomas's Hospital appears to have originated in the Priory in the 1170s and then, following a disastrous fire in 1212, to have relocated c.1213/15 on the other side of what is now Borough High Street, occupying a site which by 1240 had expanded to some nine acres. By then continuous building had stretched from the bridge to St George's parish church for some half a century. Set apart to the south, the Lock Hospital for isolation cases (*see* p73) was probably established in the 1240s.

The emergence of such significant local insti-

8.  *Visscher's view of Old London Bridge from the south west. Heads of executed people are displayed at the bridge entrance. St Mary Overie is to the left.*

tutions as the priory and hospital was overshadowed in importance by the construction of the first London Bridge to be made of stone. Credited to a priest, Peter de Colechurch, this stupendous work was commenced in 1176 and completed in 1209. Around 1200 Bridge House, the headquarters of the wardens responsible for its upkeep, was established by its southern end, with stone walls and a gated entry. As well as serving as a meeting-place for business this structure was also used as a depository for materials needed to keep the bridge in repair. An inventory of 1350 enumerates a stockpile including quantities of Portland stone, 120 elm piles, 400 oak baulks and 12,000 tiles. Equipment for bridge maintenance included two boats, two pile-drivers and three barges. London Bridge was eventually lined with shops and, complete with its own chapel, the last resting-place of its designer, became one of the wonders of medieval Europe. Until the construction of Westminster Bridge in 1738-50 it remained the only bridge over the Thames and, as such, was destined to play a major role in the history of the capital. It survived for over six centuries, only to be replaced by Rennie's bridge (now at Lake Havasu in Arizona) in 1830-31

*9. The Drawbridge Gate of Old London Bridge.*

*10. The Bridge House in the 18th century.*

## THE STATELY HOMES OF SOUTHWARK

During the twelfth and thirteenth centuries Southwark developed as a distinctly up-market residential area, the chosen location of over a dozen ecclesiastical mansions, including the London homes of the Bishops of Winchester and Rochester, the Archdeacon of Surrey, the Abbots of Hyde, Battle, Beaulieu, Waverley and St Augustine at Canterbury and the Priors of Lewes, St Swithin's, Winchester and Christ Church, Canterbury. The Warenne earls of Surrey also had a residence on Tooley Street.

The most impressive of these residences was Winchester House. King Stephen's brother, Henri de Blois (died 1171), justified this splendid establishment by reference to "the many inconveniences and losses sustained through the lack of a house of our own when called to London on royal or other business." Thomas à Becket stayed at Winchester House overnight on the momentous journey which was to take him to his martyrdom in 1170. Simon de Montfort lodged there in 1238. Able, ambitious, arrogant Peter des Roches, Bishop of Winchester from 1205 to 1238 (*see p40*), set in train a major rebuilding which included a great hall with walls over three feet thick, set at first floor level over a vaulted cellar. Apart from extensive gardens and stables, the complex would also one day have its own tennis court and separate lock-ups for male and female prisoners. Another of its most striking features was the 'great gutter', a covered drain of dressed stone, big enough for a man to crawl through. In the fourteenth century further alterations would be undertaken by royal architect Henry Yevele and a great rose window inserted. Despite

11.  *Part of Hollar's view of London Bridge, showing the southern end.*

12. *Winchester House c.1649, from the tower of St Saviour's church.*

successive enlargements of the building its park remained substantial. As late as 1457 this was still being cropped for fodder and tree lopping and used to pasture a couple of dozen sheep.

Inventories and accounts reveal that the stables of Winchester House normally contained over fifty horses, the library possessed no less than twenty-six books, the larder was stacked with exotic imported foodstuffs such as figs, dates and rice and house-guests sat down to table with knives whose handles were made of jasper, crystal and ivory. In 1406 Edmund, Earl of Kent, married the sister of the Duke of Milan in the priory church and held his wedding reception in Winchester House afterwards. In 1559 John, Duke of Finland, was received there in state, the walls festooned with sumptuous hangings of arras, shot with silk, silver and gold. Queen Elizabeth dined there in 1577. The last episcopal resident was the saintly Lancelot Andrewes, who died there in 1626. During the Commonwealth period the former episcopal palace was used to hold royalist prisoners, such as the scholarly naval hero and crypto-Catholic Sir Kenelm Digby (1603-65).

## THE DOWNSIDE

Despite its array of impressive edifices, until the mid-thirteenth century much of Southwark retained a semi-rural air. The grounds of Winchester House were originally used to raise rye, barley and vegetables, while reeds, nettles and willow loppings were sold off as cash crops. Later, vines were planted and grain crops were abandoned in favour of fruit, nuts and herbs. In the early thirteenth century the episcopal residence was still functioning as an agricultural depot, receiving massive deliveries – 106,000 herrings, 306 pigs – from outlying estates. Only a small proportion of these products was for immediate consumption, most being intended for sale, charitable disposal or onward transmission.

Efforts were made at this time to stabilise the river shoreline, with revetments made of recycled materials, ranging from ship's timbers to old wheelbarrows. These retained beds of crushed chalk, laid over the layers of peat created by periodic inundations. Bankside seems to have originated as a causeway constructed in this fashion in 1218-19. The Templars' manor to the west of this feature was subject to recurrent flood-

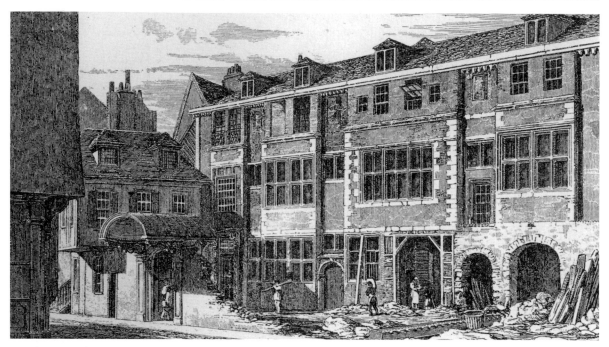

13.  *Remains of Winchester House, which survived until the nineteenth century.*

ing and its buildings consequently remained in generally poor condition. Elsewhere along the shoreline, however, the tidal Thames did useful work, powering four tidemills at the eastern end of Tooley Street.  By 1200 there were ten mills and by 1300 at least seventeen were known to have been in operation along or near the Southwark foreshore.

Positive development in the shape of parish churches, rich residences, river revetments and drainage ditches were offset by burgeoning nuisances, such as the noxious smells and effluents produced by activities such as tanning and lime burning.  Moral pollution was likewise already evident. What is now Park Street was already known in the thirteenth century as '*wala puellarum*' ('wall or embankment of the young girls') – translated euphemistically as 'Maiden Lane'.

## CONTRACTION AND RECOVERY

In 1324-5 feckless, reckless Edward II, enjoying the final phase of personal power of his erratic reign, had built for himself a walled and moated residence in Tooley Street, known as La Rosere or the Rosary, roughly between the present-day Hay's Galleria and Tower Bridge.  Its facilities included fish ponds, lined with chalk blocks and internally partitioned by hurdles, to keep fresh pike and eels in.

The political and financial entanglements which brought Edward to his ghastly end provided, as royal difficulties were so recurrently to do through the centuries, an opportunity for the City of London to strengthen its hand *vis-à-vis* its troublesome neighbour.  As Martha Carlin has emphasised, "to the Londoners of its own day, medieval Southwark was a headache. It was an asylum of undesirable industries and residents, a commercial rival, an administrative anachronism and a perpetual jurisdictional affront." In 1327 London acquired limited control of Crown holdings in Southwark. As an economic acquisition this was negligible but it enhanced the potential for limiting the area's more objectionable activities.

The existence of the Rosary doubtless encouraged lay magnates and gentry also to acquire residences in what had become a *quartier* of the higher clergy. Where Edward II led the Earl of Huntingdon and the Countesses of March and Pembroke followed, along with numerous knights. Their substantial homes were usually set back from the roadway and approached through gated entries, the street frontages of their holdings being lined with shops, with dwellings over, to yield useful rents. Tooley Street (then known as Short Southwark) and Borough High Street (then known as Long Southwark) became increasingly commercial, the latter boasting some two dozen inns, taverns and ale-houses, most notably the Tabard, first mentioned in 1306 and immortalised by Chaucer (*see illustrations 1,3 & 4*).

The dearth of 1315-16 gave a severely Malthusian check to population growth. Further brutal blows came with the onset of the Black Death in 1348-9 and its recurrence in 1361. The population of Southwark may have fallen by some 60%, being reduced to just over 2,000 by 1381, when the local poll tax returns provide a basis for calculation. This downturn represented an undoubted setback but proved less permanent than in many provincial cities. The King's Bench and Marshalsea prisons were both in existence by the third quarter of the fourteenth century (*see pp 76-80*). Paved streets became the rule rather than the exception in the course of the fifteenth century. By 1444 at least Southwark had a flourishing fair, recognised and regularised by a charter granted by Edward IV in 1462. This grant included the right to convene a 'Pie Powder' court (from *'pieds poudreux'* 'dusty feet') to provide on the spot settlement of disputes between merchants whose peripatetic lifestyle excluded them from the slow-moving processes of more conventional courts.

Southwark's economic and demographic recovery owed much to in-migration, both from other parts of England, from Wales and from abroad. The 'Doche' – migrants from the Low Countries and Germany – were especially prominent. The men were stereotyped as brewers, the women as bawds. There was something in this, the Anglicised Frowe (from Flemish *vrouw* – woman or wife) being a common surname among local prostitutes. But there were also significant numbers of cordwainers (makers of quality shoes), tailors and goldsmiths. By the sixteenth century the 'Doche' would assert a virtual monopoly over the glazing and printing trades and make a mark as precocious pioneers of the hi-tech arts of making spectacles and watches. A survey of aliens in the capital, conducted in 1571, totalled them at 7,143, of whom almost a tenth, 698, were domiciled in Southwark, 486 of them in the parish of St Olave's. Thus concentrated, the 'Doche' maintained a cohesive identity, marrying amongst themselves and preferentially taking each other's offspring as apprentices. They seem, however, to have been effectively integrated into the broader community, attending local churches, holding parish offices, serving on juries and contributing to local charities. There is little evidence of neighbourly xenophobia, although there was recurrent antagonism from the generality of Londoners, particularly when economic hardship sharpened pre-existing prejudices.

## ALARMS AND EXCURSIONS

During the Peasants' Revolt of 1381, when the Kentish mob led by Wat Tyler and John Ball surged through Southwark, the local stews (*see p43*) were sacked and fired and their female Flemish employees were singled out as a target for popular wrath.

In 1450 Southwark became even more significantly involved in a popular uprising when Jack Cade set up his headquarters in the White Hart Inn on 2 July. Little is certain about Cade's background except that he was Irish. He appears to have been suspected of the murder of a pregnant woman and fled to France, where he fought against the English and subsequently passed himself off as a doctor. He was probably not the original leader of the Kentish rebels who protested against the misconduct of the French war but seems to have come to the fore during their march on London.

The day after Cade set up his headquarters in the White Hart, Cade's men, reinforced by prisoners from the King's Bench and Marshalsea prisons, crossed London Bridge to seek out alleged traitors in the City but returned that night to Southwark. The body of Lord Say, beheaded in Cheapside, was dragged back naked and headless behind a horse all the way to the White Hart. Sir John Fastolfe (1378-1459), who had distinguished himself at Agincourt and spent most of the rest of his active career campaigning in France with diminishing success in the closing stages of the Hundred Years War, numbered himself among their potential victims. Cade's followers included many disenchanted ex-servicemen, bearing a grudge against former commanders, like Fastolfe. Having purchased the Rosary estate in 1446 and rebuilt the house, Fastolfe evidently lacked confidence in its drawbridge, moat and quarter-mile *enceinte* of walls and prudently retreated to the Tower.

Cade's undoing began when his personal plun-

NORTH WEST VIEW OF THE HALL OF

AS IT APPEARED AFTER THE FIRE

Total Length of the Hall, from East to West within the Walls, 108 feet 5 inches
Width of the Hall within, 30 feet 3 inches. Thickness of the Wall 3 f.t 6 inches.

WINCHESTER PALACE, SOUTHW.

WHICH HAPPENED the 28.th of AUG.t 1814.

Diameter of the Circular Window, 12 feet; each side of its Triangular
Compartments, 2 feet 8 inches.

14. *View of the Hall of Winchester Palace after the fire of 28 August 1814.*

dering led to general looting which threatened the previously sympathetic populace of the capital. Londoners reacted by mobilising their militia and securing the guns in the Tower. On the night of the 5/6 July some two hundred combatants were killed in a confused fight for control of London Bridge which ended with the rebels holding only the southern end. Exhausted, both sides agreed to a truce. Bishop Waynflete (*see p41*), accompanied by the Archbishops of Canterbury and York, risked a meeting face to face with Cade in St Margaret's church, a few steps from the White Hart. Following a royal proclamation of a general pardon for the insurrectionists the bulk of Cade's army rapidly dissolved.

Cade and his remaining followers, after further looting in Dartford, retreated into Kent. Cade himself was mortally wounded in a skirmish which led to his capture. The hostess of the White Hart subsequently identified Cade's naked corpse, which was then taken to King's Bench for dismemberment. The quartered body was paraded through Southwark and the City – with the head between the two halves of his trunk – before the head was spiked at the Southwark end of London Bridge to stare sightlessly at the scene of its owner's brief triumph. The entire bloody episode is recalled, in not quite such graphic detail, in Shakespeare's *Henry VI Part II*.

## A CHANGE OF CHARACTER

There is much evidence of a sustained and substantial rise in Southwark's population in the first half of the sixteenth century. The houses along the river-front side of Tooley Street seem to have continued in high-status occupation for a while, given such archaeological finds as pieces of armour and what may well be British's first imported banana. But four new side-turnings were developed for cheap housing off the main thoroughfare between 1481 and 1506. Elsewhere tenter-grounds (areas for stretching cloth) and gardens were built over with tenements and existing dwellings were sub-divided. Mean streets dubbed Alleys or Rents proliferated, twenty of them between 1500 and 1550, when the area's population is reckoned to have reached over 8,000, making it about one-eighth as populous as the capital as a whole.

As the Borough's inns grew in number and size the need for magnates' townhouses diminished. Lord Cobham's residence became the Green Dragon. The house in which Sir Edward Poynings (1459-1521), Privy Councillor and Garter Knight, was born, later became the Crosskeys Tavern, subsequently the Queen's Head, where John Harvard was born (*see p40*). Charles Brandon, Henry VIII's brother-in-law, ennobled as Duke of Suffolk, developed an imposing residence just opposite where the church of St George the Martyr now stands, although its days of glory were brief. In 1522 Henry VIII and the emperor Charles V were entertained there. Suffolk House was used as a mint between 1545 and 1551, but it was still habitable enough for Philip II and Queen Mary to spend a night there. Mary passed it to the Archbishop of York, who disposed of it to use the purchase price to buy property at Charing Cross. Suffolk House was then demolished piecemeal between 1557 and 1562. According to Stow the owner "sold the lead, stone, iron etc and in place thereof built many small cottages of great rents, to the increasing of beggars in that borough." The expansion of population meant that St Margaret's and St Olave's were compelled to purchase new burial grounds. The suppression of St Mary's as a priory at the Dissolution led to the fusion of the former parishes of St Margaret and St Mary Magdalene to create a new parish, St Saviour's, the former priory church becoming the largest parish church in England. The prior's house was acquired by Sir Anthony Browne, a devout Catholic who nevertheless amassed large amounts of property from the dispossessed Church. The former St Margaret's was turned over for use by the courts of Admiralty and Assize. Part of it became the Compter (*aka* the Counter), a prison for local miscreants and petty debtors. Its name was said to be a corruption of *Computare* because, according to a contemporary wag, "whosoever slippeth in there must be sure to account, and pay well too, ere he get out again." The Pope's Head patriotically restyled itself the King's Head. The St George's inn became the George. St Thomas's hospital exchanged its former affiliation with Becket for the Apostle.

As complaints about straying pigs, sanitation, street obstructions and rubbish – especially butchers' waste consisting of 'tubbes of garbyche' – were recorded with increasing frequency, official street scavengers were appointed to tackle these nuisances. Public urination was banned in 1543. The records of the Court Leet of Paris Garden show that from about 1560 punishment of misdemeanours by fines was increasingly replaced by confinement to the stocks or the cage. Lock-ups, cucking-stools and the existence of a pillory in both Tooley Stret and the High Street imply a heightened concern with public order, doubtless associated with the patrons of local archery butts, bowling alleys and, from 1546, bear-baiting rings (*see p45*). Tudor Southwark's status as a fully urbanised community was finally confirmed by the frequency and severity of its traffic-jams.

# Shakespeare's Bankside

Although Bankside became early modern London's leading theatre district it was not the first such, a distinction which went to Shoreditch. Both areas shared a factor essential to their success, being easy of access from the City proper but outside its immediate jurisdiction. Actors were memorably referred to by London's Lord Mayor in 1580 as "a very superfluous sort of men". They faced, moreover, stiff competition from many other kinds of entertainment – bear-baiting, cock-fighting and displays of tumbling, juggling, fencing and equestrianism, not to mention such free spectacles as public sermons, the exposure of malefactors in the pillory and public executions.

## THE ROSE

Bankside's first theatre was the Rose, built on a former rose garden (but possibly taking its name from a local brothel) in 1586-7. Its promoters were the versatile and none too scrupulous entrepreneur Philip Henslowe (died 1616) and John Cholmely, a grocer. Henslowe was much the more active partner. Resident in Southwark some forty years, he was variously a dealer in wood and in goat-skins, a dyer and a manufacturer of starch, a money-lender and a proprietor of inns and lodging-houses. The dubious character of the latter did not prevent him from becoming a vestryman and churchwarden at St Saviour's, where he lies buried, though his actual grave is unmarked. Grasping but shrewd, Henslowe frequently used the financial embarrassments of dramatists and authors to his own advantage. His account books constitute an invaluable source for the early history of English theatre.

Octagonal in shape, the Rose was constructed of wood and plaster and partly thatched. The identity of its first company is not known. The companies known as Strange's Men and the Admiral's Men were certainly there in 1592. Strange's Men left in 1594, the Admiral's Men went back across the river to the new Fortune theatre in 1600. It was probably at the Rose that Shakespeare's *Henry VI Part I* and *Titus Andronicus* were first performed. It was certainly there that Edward Alleyn (1566-1626) established his reputation as the leading actor of the era, notably in Marlowe's majestic dramas *Tamburlaine the Great*,

*Doctor Faustus* and *The Jew of Malta*. Over the course of its busiest three years the Rose put on fifty-five plays, including works by Ben Jonson, John Webster and Thomas Dekker. Dekker in particular was frenetically prolific. In February 1598 he was released from the Counter by Henslowe in the sum of forty shillings and repaid the debt by turning out at least eight plays between then and 1602. Like Jonson, with whom he collaborated (until they fell out for good – and ill), Dekker delighted in depicting the trickery and swindling which was commonly practised on dupes who ventured onto Bankside. Dekker did not, however, prove sufficiently street-wise himself to avoid a prolonged period of imprisonment, being incarcerated in King's Bench from 1613 to 1616.

The opening of the Globe in 1599 seems to have damaged takings at the Rose. No performances of plays are recorded there after 1603 and when the ground lease expired in 1605, the Rose was demolished. By then Henslowe's interests as a theatrical impresario were centred on the Fortune, which (modelled on the Globe) had opened in Golden Lane, Cripplegate in 1600. He retained an interest in Bankside through bear-baiting (*see p45*) in which he was in partnership with Edward Alleyn, who had married Henslowe's step-daughter Joan and thus become his son-in-law. Alleyn retired from the stage in 1603 to manage his portfolio of property and business interests. He later founded the almshouses and school now known as Dulwich College.

The foundations of the Rose were rediscovered early in 1989, near Rose Alley, just west of Southwark Bridge. Actor Patrick Stewart, of *Star Trek* fame, was among the first to attempt to interpret the implications of its dimensions:

> We're told that the Globe ... was a big house. But the Rose certainly wasn't – and Shakespeare's first plays were done for this stage ... The auditorium can't have been more than 60 feet deep ... The bricks mark the edge of the stage. Up to now we have thought that Shakespeare's actors worked on a platform projecting into the house. This shows that it curved gently into the house. An actor wouldn't be working with spectators standing behind him. He could command the house with a look.

Detailed excavation revealed that the Rose had been significantly enlarged in the course of its short history and a sloping floor had been installed to improve the groundlings' view of the stage.

15. *The Swan Theatre around 1614.*

## THE SWAN

An outbreak of plague in 1592 led to a two year ban on theatrical performances. At the same time appalling weather ruined successive harvests, driving food prices sky high and severely squeezing spare money for spending on entertainment.

The Swan was built, after the lifting of the theatrical ban in 1594, by Francis Langley, a respectable draper. It stood slightly west of Hopton Street in Paris Garden. In 1596 Johannes (Jan) de Wit, a priest from Utrecht, made a sketch of the interior and sent it to a friend, who made a copy of it. This copy is the only authenticated contemporary view of a theatre interior of the period. De Wit described the Swan enthusiastically as "the largest and most distinguished ... since it contains 3,000 persons and is built of a concrete of flint stones and supported wooden columns painted in such imitation of marble that it might deceive even the most cunning." It was long thought that an audience of 3,000 at the Swan must have been either a gross exaggeration or a simple mistake but a modern experiment involving hundreds of schoolchildren has suggested that two thousand plus adults was certainly feasible. The Swan had no regular company of its own and so often staged other attractions, such as fencing bouts. It has been sug-

16. *Interior of the Swan Theatre in 1596, drawn by Johannes de Wit.*

17.   *A contemporary drawing of the Globe Theatre.*

gested that as an active theatre the Swan lasted little longer than the short period 1596-7. It certainly fell into relative disuse after the death of Langley in 1601. In 1602 there was a riot when a promised performance of Richard Vennar's *England's Joy* was aborted at the last moment by the author's arrest. The infuriated crowd went on the rampage. Middleton's *A Chaste Maid in Cheapside* was staged at the Swan in 1611 but after the opening of the Hope in 1613 the theatre was virtually abandoned. It was last definitely known to have been used in 1621. A map of 1627 shows it as the 'olde playe house'. The latest record of its existence was in a pamphlet of 1632, in which it was described in almost poignant terms as being like a ruined fortress – "in times past as famous as any of the other ... fallen to decay and like a dying Swanne, hanging downe her head, seemed to sing her owne dierge".

## THE GLOBE

The Globe, opened in 1599, was actually 'The Theatre' recycled. It was originally constructed by builder turned actor James Burbage (?1530-97) in Shoreditch. When the lease on its site ran out the landowner, Giles Allen, expected to inherit the building along with the reversion of the land. His intention was "to pull down the same and to convert the wood and timber thereof to some better use". Burbage's son Cuthbert (?1566-1636), having carpentry as the family trade and aided by a gang of a dozen men, simply disassembled the building at dead of night and took "all the wood and timber thereof unto the Banckside in the parishe of St Mary Overyes and there erected a newe playehowse with the sayd timber and woode."

The Globe was home to the Chamberlain's Men, known from James I's reign as the King's Men, with the technical status of 'Grooms of the Chamber' to ward off harassment by disapproving aldermen and magistrates. Led by Cuthbert's actor brother Richard Burbage (1567-1619) in collaboration with William Shakespeare (1564-1616) it outshone all other companies, performing the latter's plays as they left his fluent pen. Richard Burbage himself pioneered such classic roles as Hamlet, Lear, Othello and Richard III.

Shakespeare prospered mightily from his triple role as actor, dramatist and eventually eighth-part shareholder in the venture. Having arrived in London around 1592, he was already applying for a grant of arms by 1596 and in 1597 was able to purchase the second biggest house in his home

18. *Richard Burbage, from a portrait in Dulwich College.*

town of Stratford. He was, however, doubtless greatly saddened that his success drew his younger brother Edmund up from the country to join him as 'a player' in 1607 only to die of plague within months of his arrival, aged just 28. Edmund was interred at St Saviour's on the morning of 31 December, perhaps so that the other players in the company could attend, it being normal for afternoon performances to take place indoors in the winter. Shakespeare paid extra to have a 'knell of the great bell' rung in mourning. All told the funeral cost twenty shillings, ten times as much as an average one.

As Shakespeare withdrew from writing to enjoy his fortune in retirement, his place was taken by Sir Francis Beaumont (1584-1616) and John Fletcher (1579-1625) who represented a new generation. They have been bracketed together as a more than close partnership – the seventeenth-century gossip John Aubrey alleged that they shared everything, including a mistress. In fact they can be proved to have worked together for only a few years and on half a dozen plays rather than the fifty or more which literary tradition has assigned to them. Beaumont gave up writing after his marriage in 1613. Fletcher, son of a bishop of London, was a far more active collaborator with other writers. He died of plague in the great outbreak of 1625 and was buried in St Saviour's.

Shakespeare returned to his birthplace, where he died a couple of years later and was buried. Whether he ever actually lived on Bankside remains a matter of scholarly dispute; in the absence of confirmatory documentation 'not proven' must remain the verdict. This has not prevented St Saviour's from claiming him as a parishioner and thus installing in his memory an elaborate stained-glass window (1954) and a monument (1912) of the reclining Bard, memorably described by architectural critic Ian Nairn as "a gelid apparition ... in some astonishing stone which looks exactly like frozen aspic or frog-spawn, very creepy."

The Globe burned down in two hours or less in 1613 when a stage cannon set fire to its thatched roof during a performance of *Henry VIII*. Given that there were only two narrow exits it struck contemporaries as little less than miraculous that there was no major loss of life. Sir Henry Wotton reported to a friend with evident glee that "only one man had his breeches set on fire, that would perhaps have broiled him, if he had not by the benefit of a provident wit put it out with Bottle-Ale."

Reconstructed in 1614 (with a tiled roof instead of thatch), the Globe saw the first production of Webster's horrific revenge tragedy *The Duchess of Malfi*. In 1623 the actors and former business managers of the company Condell and Hemming, having appointed themselves literary executors of their former colleague's departed genius, triumphantly produced the celebrated 'First Folio' of Shakespeare's works. Philip Massinger (1583-1640) took over as the main dramatist. He is best remembered for the satiric *A New way to Pay Old Debts*, produced around 1625. Massinger was succeeded by James Shirley (1596-1666), who excelled at comedy and had the satisfaction of seeing his works revived by the next generation of actors at the Restoration. The Globe remained in business until the suppression of theatres on the outbreak of the civil war in 1642. It was demolished in 1644 and tenements put up on its site.

## THE HOPE
Following the destruction of the Globe in 1613 Philip Henslowe in partnership with one Jacob Meade, doubtless thinking to take advantage of

19.  *The Hope Theatre.*

an anticipated gap in the market, had converted his bear-baiting arena to become the Hope, fitting it with a movable stage.

Instructions to his carpenter reveal that Henslowe took the Swan as his model and required the use of durable oak, not cheap 'fur'. In 1614 Jonson's *Bartholomew Fair* was given its premiere there. After 1616, the year of Henslowe's death, there is no record of plays being staged, though bear-baiting continued until its suppression under the Commonwealth forty years later. The building, however, seems to have been still standing in 1682-3. Part of the site, only two hundred yards from the Globe, was rediscovered under a car park in March 2001. The rest lies under four properties, making public display impossible.

## THE DREAM

Sam Wanamaker (1919-93) established the Globe Playhouse Trust in 1970 to raise funds for the reconstruction of the Globe. A refugee from the McCarthyite persecution in the 1950s, Chicago-born Wanamaker settled in England to pursue a successful career as an actor and director It was his drive and vision which led to the ultimate realisation of his dream in the face of apathy, scepticism and downright hostility. Remarkably, the true site of the Globe was rediscovered in the autumn of 1989, a few months after the uncovering of the site of the Rose. Sam Wanamaker was awarded an honorary doctorate by the University of London and appointed CBE, but died before the Globe reconstruction was completed. A modest but handsome plaque, next to the Shakespeare memorial, honours his memory in Southwark Cathedral. His lasting monument is, of course, the reconstructed Globe itself.

*21. The Falcon Tavern on Bankside as it appeared in 1805.*

*20. Houses on Bankside, 1827, from a drawing by Buckler in the Guildhall Library.*

# Second City

### EXPANSION AND DECLINE

Between the Reformation of the 1530s and the 'Glorious Revolution' of 1688 the character of Southwark changed decisively and dramatically, from fashionable faubourg to suburban slum. The forcible eviction of the great ecclesiastics, followed by the voluntary migration of their aristocratic neighbours, was one initial cause of this transformation. Another was the huge expansion of the population of the metropolis as a whole, compounded by a local influx of refugees, mainly from the Low Countries. From a population of some 10,000 at the beginning of Elizabeth I's reign Southwark almost doubled to 19,000 by its end. By the outbreak of the civil wars the population had risen by over fifty per cent – despite major plague epidemics in 1577-8, 1603, 1634-7 and 1641.

A further disruptive factor was the jurisdictional ambiguity which confused the enforcement of order and morality in the locality. In 1550 the City of London paid Edward VI for the residue of his manorial rights in the Southwark area and re-constituted their acquisition as the Bridge Ward Without. This transaction did not, however, confer authority over the Liberties of the Mint and Clink or the Manor of Paris Garden. Nor did it prevent continual challenges from the justices of Surrey, who continued to claim involvement in many judicial and administrative matters, such as holding musters of the local militia. In 1596 the City's Court of Aldermen felt impelled to appoint one William Cleybrooke as a special Marshal with orders to apprehend "all manner of rogues, beggars, idle and vagrant persons within the borough of Southwark and the liberties thereof."

The result of these various cross-pressures and institutional interests, as Reilly and Marshall observe, was that "a piecemeal and highly complex system of administration developed, which involved the City, the manorial authorities, the parishes, the county of Surrey and, in the eighteenth and nineteenth centuries, specially formed bodies for particular purposes", such as Commissioners for Sewers, Paving, Lighting and Watching (i.e. police) and later for Burials, Baths and Libraries.

The problematic status of law enforcement in the locality attracted pursuits, pastimes, profes-

22. *The White Hart Inn, c1870.*

sions and people which might nowadays be variously classified as immoral, anti-social, subversive or environmentally obnoxious. As Dekker, no stranger to the area, observed with literary bravura – "how happy therefore were cities if they had no suburbs, since they serve but as caves, where monsters are bred up to devour the cities themselves!"

23. *The Queen's Head drawn by T.R.Way, 1896.*

24. *The Catherine Wheel Inn, 1840.*

25. *A courtyard typical of the old Borough High Street; the building on the left is the former Goat Inn c.1542.*

Dekker also described bustling Borough High Street in the early seventeenth century as "a continued ale house with not a shop to be seen." If this sounds like hyperbole consider that in 1631 the Surrey JPs recorded a staggering 238 alehouses in Southwark and Kent Street, of which the licences of 43 had already been withdrawn. In that same year, in the Great Liberty manor alone, a hundred fines of one shilling were imposed on alehouse keepers for giving false measure. An excess of alehouses was held to encourage not only excessive tippling but also to provide convenient venues for gambling, muggings, prostitution, the fencing of stolen goods and conspiracies against church and state – "nests of Satan where the owls of impiety lurk and where all evil is hatched ...". Like theatres, they were also thought to serve as breeding-grounds for physical as well as moral contagions.

26. *Overhanging houses in Borough High Street.*

## STOW'S SOUTHWARK

John Stow, the capital's first true historian, re-alised that, whatever its downside, Southwark was a prodigious source of revenue as well as trouble, asserting in his 1598 *Survey of London* that "this borough yieldeth about ... eight hundred pounds which is more than any one city in England payeth, except London." But Stow was also acutely aware of the changes in population and amenity which had altered the capital so markedly in his own lifetime. Winchester House he praised as "a very fair house, well repaired." But he also noted that the adjoining former residence of the Bishop of Rochester had become ruinous and that where the "large and most sumptuous" Suffolk House had once stood, now there were "many small cottages at great rents, to the increasing of beg-gars in that borough." The former residence of the Abbot of St Augustine's, Canterbury had likewise been sub-divided into tenements. By Stow's day the former dwelling of the Prior of St Swithin was in ruins; by 1649 it had been patched up for sub-letting as thirty-seven resi-dential units. The Prior of Lewes' home had become the Walnut Tree tavern and the Abbot of Battle's the Flower de Luce (Fleur de lys). Local businessman William Emerson, owner of the Spur Inn in Borough High Street, bought the precincts of the former St Margaret's church in 1555 and squeezed nine tenements in there. Emerson's impressive monument in Southwark Cathedral nevertheless proclaims with smug simplicity that he "Lived and died an Honest Man". His son Thomas (died 1595) founded a parish charity and is remembered in the name of Emerson Street. American philosopher Ralph Waldo Emerson was allegedly among his more remote descendants. Just north of St Mary's, where Viscount Montague had occupied the former priory house and briefly employed Guy Fawkes to wait on him at table, the once imposing residence became a pothouse; its garden was to be cleared in 1625 to make way for "meane cottages and habitacions for the poorer sort of people that crouded themselves together theare." Later the sixty homes and four wharves would be neighbours to a soapworks and pottery kilns (*see p93*). The general growth of London as a whole, as well as the influx of incomers, led to an extensive subdivision of houses which caused alarm amongst those who were decently housed. In 1598 the Privy Council recorded that:

> Complaint hath been made ... by divers inhab-itants ... in the Burroughe of Southwark ... that certain persons of wealthe thorought [sic] the covetous dispocion of certain persons have of late yeres not onlie converted faire and large dwelling-houses into tenements with raysing of great rent of the same, but where manie of them being of good habiillyte did inhabit those houses, and did paie all duties besides and other chardges with the rest of the paryshioners, now in their roomes are placed many poore people that have releefe from the parish, where the landlord reapeth great rents for small cottages and are subject to no chardg with the parish ...

Open space did survive further south. John Gerard (1545-1612), collecting specimens for his famous *Herbal* in the 1590s, recorded "Of water violets I have not found such plenty in any place as in the water ditches adjoining to saint George his fielde ..." A map of Paris Garden Manor dated to 1627 shows that, except along the river front itself, the area remained largely undeveloped. Its dilapidated manor house had become a gambling den or worse (*see p44*). But much of the open land was designated as 'witsters ground', used for bleaching cloths or drying washing which was then parcelled up in 'fowlding houses'. In 1655 the area was still reckoned to have fifty acres of meadow, twenty of pasture and twenty or-chards.

## SIN AND STABILITY

Jeremy Boulton's painstaking study of seventeenth-century Southwark reveals a community which was, despite being part of a bustling port, and despite a sometimes startling local level of inter-personal violence, still quite surprisingly stable in terms of its core community – a finding much at variance with contemporary condemnations of the area as a den of vice, populated by the entire spectrum of metropolitan low-life – "Daunters, Fydlers and Minstrels, Diceplayers, Maskers, Fencers, Bearwardes, Theeves, Common Players in Enterludes, Cutpurses, Cosiners, Maisterless servauntes, Jugglers, Roges, sturdye Beggers etc." Beyond the condemnations of the moralist lurked the apprehensions of the servants of the state, that roguish riff-raff might provide a convenient cloak for far worse threats to the polity – "masterless men, out of service ... Irishmen, Papists, and such like, lately come from beyond the sea, and from the service of her Majesty's enemies". In 1594 special agent William Gardiner reported that he had been "informed by the constables and other inhabitants that they abide for the most part about Southwark, where they give much trouble."

Boulton's analysis of Southwark's local householders as they were in 1609 shows, however, that nearly half had lived in the same house for five years and almost a third for ten years. Of the remainder a third had either died or moved locally. Four fifths had married someone from within their own or an immediately adjoining parish. Generalised stability did not, however, necessarily imply general prosperity. In 1622 only two-thirds of householders were sufficiently well-off to pay rates and a tenth of the local populace was being supported by relief from the parish. In the commercially peripheral riverside districts of Paris Garden and the Clink some 40% of the working population were watermen of one sort or another, a precarious trade, accident-prone and dependent on the weather and seasons. Small households, averaging 3.8 persons were the norm. There were many poor widows and a high level of child mortality. There was also a perhaps disproportionately large number of apprentices. Young, male, with little disposable income but surrounded by temptations purveyed on a commercial scale, they constituted an ever-present potential for disorder.

*27. One of the forts, located near today's Tabard Street, erected by Parliament for the defence of London during the Civil War. The river Effra flows in the forefront down to the Thames.*

## FORTS AND FIRES

Demographic disturbances, arising from disease or migration, were matched by intermittently dramatic transformations to the physical structures of the neighbourhood.

During the civil wars of the 1640s the entire capital, north and south of the river, was surrounded by a huge *enceinte* of earthen and wood ramparts, punctuated with over twenty forts. Two stood in St George's Fields. The larger, located where the Imperial War Museum now stands, could accommodate a garrison of three thousand men. Within a decade these fortifications had been totally demolished and virtually disappeared.

In 1632 fire broke out on London Bridge, destroying dozens of houses. Failure to reconstruct these created a natural fire-break which helped to save Southwark from the terrible fire that devastated the City of London in 1666. In 1676, however, Southwark was itself visited by a hugely destructive outbreak which began in a local oilshop. The diminutive but valiant Lord Craven (1606-97) took charge of fire-fighting operations, with the assistance of Charles II's bastard son, the handsome, popular James Scott, Duke of Monmouth (1649-85). Craven, Lord Lieutenant of Surrey, was still an inveterate firefighter at seventy, and thus combined public duty with private avocation. Despite such illustrious attentions, however, over five hundred houses were lost. This devastation of northern Southwark necessitated widespread rebuilding but did nothing to check the growth of population, which reached 32,000 by 1680. Another serious fire in 1689, starting in a stationer's opposite King's Bench prison, destroyed a further 180 houses – "the Buildings, being timber for the most part, and generally old, with many intricate Alleys running backward, the Flame, driven on by the Wind raged extremely".

## TENEMENTS AND TENTER-GROUNDS

The intensification of commercial and industrial activity in the locality increased pressure on residential and leisure space. Winchester House had already been let out as tenements after the Restoration and its park leased out for building in 1663. Paris Garden was built over by the end of the seventeenth century. Collier's Rents was built over two former bowling greens. In the course of the eighteenth century poor Irish migrants became an established element of the local population. Southwark's days as a desirable residential *quartier* for higher clergy and courtiers had become a very distant memory indeed. Strype in 1720 described Blackman Street as "broad, but

28. *The manor of Paris Garden, 1749.*

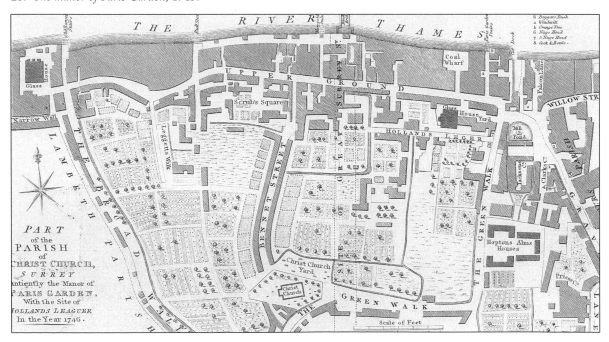

29.   *The obelisk and turnpike at St George's Fields, 1813.*

30.   *The Elephant and Castle turnpike and toll-gate, 1830.*

31. *School for the Indigent Blind at St George's Fields, fronted by the obelisk raised in honour of Brass Crosby. The Bethlem Hospital is in the distance to the right.*

the Buildings and Inhabitants not much boasted of." Professor Roy Porter has noted "the contrast between north and south banks was total. Around 1700 there was only stinking industry – distilleries, rope-works, tanneries, shambles and shipyards, south of the Thames, punctuated with bear-baiting and bawdy-houses, hogs and fogs."

This is perhaps a little harsh. Rocque's map of 1746 shows that there were still nine tentergrounds in the Bankside area alone. Even if they ought to be regarded as semi-industrial rather than recreational in character they still represented open space among crowded surroundings. A windmill could still be seen in St George's

the more up-market name of King Street in 1774; it is now Newcomen Street. Union Street was laid out between 1774 and 1781 in connection with the erection of a new workhouse there. Thomas Lant began the construction of the street which bears his name around 1770, though it was not completed until 1800. Robert Mylne (*see p108*) constructed St George's Circus and its surrounding road layout in double quick time between 1769 and 1771, stabilising the marshy sub-structure with seventy thousand cartloads of rubbish and adorning the Circus with a handsome obelisk bearing the name of the current Lord Mayor, Brass Crosby. There was perhaps more to this dedication than the mere temporal coincidence of the man, the office and the project because at the very time that Mylne was briskly supervising his army of bog-battling labourers (sub-contracted at 1s 8d per day per man to include the cost of their tools and beer) Crosby (1725-93) was at the heart of a political maelstrom which pitted Parliament itself against the City's chief magistrate as a defender of the Press. As such Lord Mayor Crosby endured imprisonment in the Tower but doggedly refused to capitulate. The eventual outcome was a triumphant and permanent vindication of the right of the press to report parliamentary debates, with Crosby duly hailed as the hero of the hour.

The construction of Mylne's Blackfriars Bridge led to the development of its main approach road as Great Surrey Street, now Blackfriars Road, between 1765 and 1790. This in turn stimulated the building of the Surrey Chapel (*see p88*), the Rotunda (*see p63*) and the Albion Mills (*see p109*), the opening of Dolben Street (then George Street) in 1776, the laying out of Stamford Street by stages between 1790 and 1815 and the building of West Square from 1791 onwards and of Nelson Square between 1807 and 1814. James Smith penned an appropriate elegy for departed Elysium in 1813:

> Saint George's fields are fields no more;
> The trowel supersedes the plough;
> Swamps, huge and inundate of yore,
> Are changed to civic villas now."

Fields until 1773. Pony races and militia musters were held on this extensive if sometimes noisome area and it served as a convenient overnight camping ground for itinerant showmen.

The eighteenth century certainly witnessed some improving projects. From 1736 onwards Ax and Bottle Yard was sufficiently built up to adopt

Regrettably it didn't quite work out like that. As the various philanthropic organisations (*see pp56-7*) departed St George's Fields from the early years of Victoria's reign the area became notorious for poor quality housing run up by speculative developers like the Hedger family (*see p49*)

# Cockney Cathedral

The present day Southwark Cathedral was fondly described in 1966 by the incomparable Ian Nairn as "a proper working cathedral …The most memorable thing about the building is the intangible contribution of a friendly and unsanctimonious atmosphere, just what a cockney cathedral ought to be." As an architectural critic and historian Nairn might, perhaps, also have mentioned that after Westminster Abbey, Southwark Cathedral is the largest medieval Gothic church in London – and that much of its Gothic fabric is even older than the Abbey's, though, as the cathedral's historian, Florence Higham, wryly noted "its fabric was to suffer through the centuries as much from its friends as from its enemies."

## ST MARY'S

Southwark Cathedral has been a cathedral only since 1905. It may be the fourth house of worship to occupy its present site. A legend recorded by Stow and fancifully elaborated in the eighteenth century, holds that the first church was established in 606, which would make it within two years of the alleged founding of the first St Paul's on the opposite side of the river. The founder was said to have been one Mary (*not* a Saxon name), daughter of a ferryman, John Overs – hence the common name of the church as St Mary Overie. Alternatively the title is said to derive from its location over the river from the City.

The Saxon minster, thought to have existed in pre-Conquest Southwark and noted in Domesday, has been attributed to the celebrated St Swithun, Bishop of Winchester (852-62), who was certainly known as a prolific builder.

The third church was constructed in the first decade of the twelfth century as part of a priory

32. *St Mary Overie church, drawn by Wenceslaus Hollar in 1661.*

33. *The gateway of St Mary's Priory.*

of Augustinian canons. Unlike monks, who pursued a life apart from the wider community, its canons dedicated themselves to pastoral service through preaching, teaching and healing – hence the emergence of St Thomas's hospital (*see p66*). Of this original priory church only fragments survive, such as the internal arch of the doorway in the north aisle and a section of blind arcading in the south aisle, to the left of the entrance. The rest was destroyed in a great fire in 1212.

Reconstruction seems to have extended over a century. In 1260 the building appears to have been deemed fit enough to host the consecration of a bishop of London, but in 1273 indulgences of thirty days were being offered in return for contributions to the fabric, and in 1303 the prior pleaded with Edward I not to wish a pensioner on him because the church had been "for thirty years a ruin" – possibly a reference to repeated

flood damage. Fire inflicted further damage in the late fourteenth century. Much of this was made good through the beneficence of Cardinal Beaufort (*see pp40-1*) and it was during his bishopric that the six bells were recast and two new ones added in 1424, quite possibly to coincide with the marriage of James I of Scotland and Beaufort's niece, Joan. In 1469, however, the stone-vaulted roof of the nave collapsed and a wooden one was substituted. A number of the carved roof-bosses, variously humorous and grotesque, can be seen at the north-western end of the church. Around 1520 Bishop Richard Foxe, founder of Corpus Christi College, Oxford, donated the great altar screen and completed the tower. The present incumbents of the screen's many niches, however, date from 1905 onwards and denote saints and kings with whom some association can be claimed.

## ST SAVIOUR'S

The priory of St Mary's was suppressed in 1539 in the closing phase of the dissolution of the monasteries. The church then became the focal point of a new parish of St Saviour's, formed by the amalgamation of the small parishes of St Margaret's and St Mary Magdalene and governed by a Corporation of Wardens, whose existence is commemorated in the name of Wardens Grove, now a cul-de-sac continuation of America Street. The conventual buildings to the north of the church were allowed to decay or were acquired by royal standard-bearer Sir Anthony Browne, whose son, a subsequent occupant, became Viscount Montague – hence Montague Close. Under Mary Tudor there was a brief Catholic counter-attack as Bishop Stephen Gardiner held a consistory court in the retro-choir, trying and condemning seven Protestants as heretics. Under Elizabeth I the retro-choir was leased out to a baker, who kept pigs there.

In 1614 the parishioners of St Saviour's, including local entrepreneur and impresario Philip Henslowe (*see p22*), clubbed together to buy St Saviour's from James I, a monarch ever-pressed for cash, for £800. Perhaps Henslowe was also present when in 1616 preacher Sutton used his pulpit to denounce those "who dishonour God … by penning and acting of plays." As if to assert their proprietorial rights wealthy members of the congregation began to be buried beneath imposing monuments which can still be seen – Alderman Richard Humble (1616), ancestor of the earls of Dudley, John Trehearne, porter to the king (1618), John Bingham (1625) and Lady Clarke (1633).

St Saviour's escaped significant vandalism during the civil wars. Pepys, who often took a leisurely 'short-cut' from his Seething Lane office to the court at Westminster by going via the southern shore, valued its tranquillity. In July 1663 he noted in his diary "I spent half an hour in St. Mary Overy's church, where are fine monuments of great antiquity." In 1680 the church was beautified by the impressive candelabrum which still dominates the nave, a gift of Dorothy Applebee, whose generosity also founded a parochial school. In 1689 the tower was completed in its present form, surmounted by four crocketed pinnacles in the style of the late fourteenth century.

Further impressive memorials continued to be added by prosperous parishioners. Local pharmacist Lionel Lockyer's, which struck Ian Nairn as being made of some substance "like *papier mâché* or melted golf-balls", advertised his patent cures in verse. Others were erected for Richard Blisse (1703), the Revd Thomas Jones (1710) and Thomas Cole (1715). Dating from a later generation is the tribute to Abraham Newland (1730-1807), located in the south choir aisle. Southwark-born Newland entered the service of the Bank of England at the age of eighteen and rose to become Chief Cashier. So conscientious that he slept at the Bank for twenty-five years, he was betrayed by a trusted deputy who embezzled funds placed by Newland in his care. As a result Newland refused an annuity offered by the Directors in recognition of his loyalty - though he did accept a service of silver plate and managed to leave a fortune of £200,000.

A major restoration of the building was undertaken by local architect George Gwilt the Younger (*see p109*) in 1822. The chapel of St Mary Magdalene was demolished but the retro-choir was carefully restored, *gratis*. Appropriately, it became Gwilt's last resting-place. Gwilt's loving labours were ill-rewarded by fate. In 1831 the nave roof fell in and in 1838 the nave itself had to be demolished, creating a void filled by "a hideous nondescript structure", which was denounced by Pugin (*see p82*) "as vile a preaching place as ever disgraced the nineteenth century."

## FROM CHURCH TO CATHEDRAL

In 1877 Southwark was transferred from the see of Winchester to the see of Rochester as part of an overall revision of diocesan boundaries to take some account of the dramatic demographic changes of the Victorian era. It fell therefore to the energetic Bishop Thorold of Rochester (1825-95) to raise funds for the restoration of St Saviour's. The foundation stone of the new nave was laid in 1890 and reconstruction commenced by the Southwark firm of Rider & Son to the designs of Sir Arthur Blomfield, the Bank of England's official architect. A new west window by Henry Holliday was inserted in 1893. The work was completed in 1897 and a new organ installed that same year.

The story of the church remained, of course, much more than the story of its structure. St Saviour's serviced a mission hall in Redcross Street and offered a wide range of activities for the local community, which were as much practical as devotional – Bible classes, sewing meetings, a penny bank, a library, a Band of Hope, a mothers' meeting and a 'Girls' Friendly Lodge'.

34.  *The High Altar of Southwark Cathedral c.1910.*

## JOHN HARVARD

In 1907 the former Chapel of St John the Evangelist was reconstructed as the Harvard chapel, thanks to the generosity of Harvard alumni. Its stained-glass window, designed by American artist John La Farge, was presented by former US ambassador James Choate, himself a Harvard graduate. John Harvard (1607-38), chief benefactor of the college named in his honour, had been baptised in St Saviour's. His mother, Katherine (née Rogers) owned the Queen's Head in Borough High Street, his father, a local butcher, having died in the plague epidemic of 1625. Katherine remarried but her second husband died within a year and so she married again, her third husband being Richard Yarwood, MP for Southwark. Her will divided the considerable estate she had accumulated through marriage between her two sons, John receiving the Queen's Head as part of his portion. Harvard emigrated to New England in 1637, taking with him over three hundred books, a huge personal library by contemporary standards. Wealthy, learned and pious, he almost immediately became a leading citizen of Charlestown, Massachusetts but succumbed to illness within a year. By his will Harvard left half his fortune, plus his books, towards the erection of a college for which the

*35. The Harvard Chapel, c.1910.*

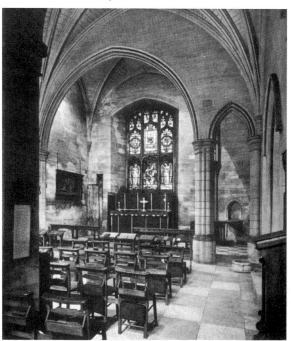

township had already pledged £400. Thanks to his benefaction work commenced forthwith and the remembrance of his generosity was perpetuated for posterity in its name.

## PRIDE AND PIETY

Whereas the priors of St Mary Overie are for the most part shadowy figures, of whom little more than names and dates of tenure is known, the bishopric of Winchester, and therefore the occupancy of Winchester House, has been held by some of the most prominent figures in English ecclesiastical history. A few whose careers significantly impinged on the present cathedral are noted here.

William Giffard (died 1129) introduced the Cistercian order to England, founding their first house at Waverley, near Farnham and supported the establishment of the Augustinian priory of St Mary Overie. His successor Henry of Blois (died 1171), brother of King Stephen, is credited with beginning the building of Winchester House. Battling bishop Peter des Roches (died 1238) served as tutor to the future Henry III, introduced the friars to England and enlarged the episcopal palace. Aymer de Valence (died 1260), grasping Poitevin half-brother to Henry III, was imposed on the see by royal *diktat*, despite the fact that he was only an acolyte and spoke no English. A contemporary chronicler noted that his death came "to the great joy of the English people."

William of Wykeham (1324-1404) was Bishop of Winchester for almost forty years, from 1367 until his death. Having served the Crown as Clerk of Works at Windsor and on diplomatic missions, he was ordained in the chapel of Winchester Palace at Southwark in 1362 and held office as Chancellor of England from 1367 to 1371. Wykeham is chiefly remembered as the founder of New College, Oxford and its 'feeder' school, Winchester College. The main object of these foundations was to remedy the catastrophic shortfall of well-educated priests created by the disastrous visitations of the Black Death in 1348-9 and 1361 – the latter of which had brought him prebendal rights and incomes at over a dozen houses of worship.

Henry Beaufort (died 1447), orthodox rather than pious, was the epitome of a proud prince of the church. The second son of John of Gaunt by his mistress Katherine Swynford, Beaufort was retrospectively legitimised and rose rapidly in the service of church and state – Chancellor of Oxford in 1397, Bishop of Lincoln in 1398. With the accession of his half-brother as Henry IV the following year he served briefly as Chancellor (1403-4) before being translated to the see of Winchester. A close confidant of the future Henry V, Beaufort was once again appointed Chancellor on his accession and subsequently became god-father to the future Henry VI. A master of financial manipulations, Beaufort played a crucial role in subsidising the French wars and also sponsored much building, including the reconstruction of the south transept of Southwark cathedral, where his coat of arms can still be seen. Appointed Chancellor a third time during the infancy of Henry VI, Beaufort attracted much local unpopularity in London, partly on account of his alleged partiality to the Flemings. Threatening notices were nailed to the doors of the episcopal palace and Beaufort gave up his office to deepen his involvement in European power politics. Elevated to Cardinal in 1427, and tipped as a possible Pope, he crowned Henry VI King of France in Paris in 1431 and was present at the burning of Joan of Arc. Beaufort's later years were devoted to pursuing some peaceful means of extricating England from the bloody and costly mire of the French wars but his chances of success were blighted by his dual loyalty to Pope and Crown. Ultimately it cost him the Papacy while sacrificing any effective influence he might have exerted over English policy.

William Waynflete (?1395-1486) was educated at Winchester and was almost certainly a fellow of New College, as well as being a protégé of Beaufort, whom he succeeded as Bishop of Winchester. Waynflete played a dramatic part in the dispersal of Cade's rebels in 1450 (*see p20*) but is chiefly remembered as the founder of Magdalen College, Oxford. As the executor of the will of Sir John Fastolf (*see p19*), he blithely diverted the old soldier's bequest for a college to be founded at Caistor in Norfolk to the benefit of his own foundation at Oxford.

Richard Foxe (?1448-1528) was a most trusted counsellor to Henry VII, patron of Wolsey and founder of Corpus Christi College, Oxford.

The last episcopal resident of Winchester House, Lancelot Andrewes (1555-1626), was distinguished as a brilliant scholar, a subtle theologian, a zealous Protestant and an able administrator. Ascetic to the point of endangering his own health, Andrewes was also fair-minded, humorous and generous. He devoted every morning to study and was said to have mastered fifteen languages. He was above all renowned as an "angel in the

*36. Lancelot Andrewes, Bishop of Winchester 1619-26.*

pulpit", much given to verbal fireworks which brought him rapid promotion under the bookish James I, who made him successively Bishop of Chichester, Ely and Winchester. Thanks to Andrewes' immense learning and linguistic expertise the king entrusted him with co-ordinating the production of his Authorised Bible. Andrewes was also sworn of the Privy Council but, against general expectation, not translated to Canterbury. T.S. Eliot rated Andrewes' sermons as ranking "with the finest English prose of their time" and drew on his *Of the Nativitie* for the opening of his own celebrated poem *Journey of the Magi*. Apart from the eleven volumes of his collected works, Andrewes is memorialized in a fine tomb at the eastern end of Southwark cathedral.

## TURBULENT PRIEST

Henry Sacheverell (1674-1724) achieved a notoriety out of all proportion to his talent. After an unspectacular but not uncomfortable academic career at Magdalen College, Oxford, where he was a friend of Joseph Addison, he was appointed chaplain of St Saviour's in 1705. Sacheverell's qualifications for the pulpit were a commanding presence and a good voice, rather than profound

*37. The tomb of Bishop Lancelot Andrewes, 1555-1626.*

learning or deep spirituality. A High Church Tory, Sacheverell, as both preacher and pamphleteer, excoriated dissenters and Whigs so abusively that in 1710 he was impeached before the House of Lords itself. On the third day of his trial the London mob rose in his support, burning and looting half a dozen dissenting chapels. The historian Bishop Burnet, then living in Clerkenwell, recorded in wonderment that "before my door one with a spade cleft the skull of another because he would not shout for Sacheverell." Although Sacheverell's printed sermons were ordered to be burned by the hangman, he was himself let off with the mildest of reproofs, a three year ban from the pulpit, much to the delight of the mob, whose hero he had become. In 1713 Queen Anne awarded him the rich living of St Andrew's, Holborn, where he quarrelled with his parishioners. Perceptive contemporaries dismissed him as a vain, ignorant, boastful adventurer. He is nonetheless honoured with a memorial window in today's Cathedral.

## PRACTICAL PRELATES

C.R. Sumner (1790-1874), who had the perhaps unenviable distinction of being chosen by George IV as his spiritual counsellor, at least benefited from the relationship to become Bishop of Winchester at the age of thirty-seven. A well-practised urbanity did not disqualify him from an energetic performance of his duties and an effective concern for the plight of the poor. In 1845 Sumner established a special fund to support schools and churches in the Southwark area. He subsequently disposed of the Southwark Park estate for cash which he used to improve the benefices of poorer clergy.

Edward Stuart Talbot (1844-1934), scion of an ancient and distinguished line, had to leave Charterhouse on account of delicate health but went on to take a double first at Oxford and lived to ninety. Appointed first warden of Keble College, Oxford, Talbot also became a prime mover in establishing Lady Margaret Hall as an Anglican college for women. After six very different years as a vicar in Leeds, he became Bishop of Rochester in 1895. Taking up residence in South London, which had been transferred from Winchester to Rochester in 1877, he was instrumental in creating a separate diocese of Southwark, of which he became first bishop in 1905. In 1911 he became Bishop of Winchester but his monument is in Southwark. Cyril Forster Garbett (1875-1955), the son of a vicar, despite painful shyness, became President of the Oxford Union. A slave to self-discipline, he served from 1919 to 1932 as Bishop of Southwark, deemed by his obituarist as "notoriously the most exacting of all English dioceses". Realising after some six years in post that he had yet to consecrate a single new church, Garbett made it his special mission to establish churches for the sprawling, barren post-war housing estates going up throughout the area in his charge. He raised £100,000 in just three years, while continuing to perform the full range of his normal episcopal duties and also serving as first chairman of the religious advisory committee of the BBC. Garbett was subsequently translated to the archbishopric of York, wrote three thoughtful books on the condition of the Church of England and in old age took advantage of the new era of cheap air travel to become an enthusiastic globetrotter, hailed for a peculiarly English spirituality – "the personification of good sense tempered by sanctity".

# Pleasure and Leisure

## THE BANKSIDE STEWS

Prostitution in England has seldom been openly approved by officialdom but it has been indirectly acknowledged. In medieval times ports especially, like Sandwich, Southampton and Hull, accepted prostitution *de facto*. In – or rather out of – most cities it was marginalized, topographically as well as socially, to fringe areas – like Southwark. As early as 1162 Henry II promulgated 'Ordinances touching upon the government of the stews in Southwark', which apparently referred to an institution already long established. The term 'stews', may be a pun, since the word described a fish-pond as well as a brothel, both of which were to be found along Bankside. Stew may be derived from the French *estuve* (whence English stove), hence bathhouse, frequently a cover for the provision of even more intimate services. The Bankside stews stood mostly on land leased from the bishop of Winchester but there was at least one, known as the Unicorn, which stood on adjoining land owned by the Prioress of Stratford-at-Bow, the probable origi-

*38. A brothel in Elizabethan times. 'In the fields and suburbs of the cities they have gardens ... walled round about very high, with their arbours and bowers fit for the purpose.'*

nal for Chaucer's fashion-conscious pilgrim. Large numbers of pottery money-boxes have been found in this area. It is surmised that these contained tips or takings collected over a period of time and were smashed open periodically to share out the contents. The City of London purged itself of prostitutes in the 1270s and again in the 1380s, driving them into outlying areas such as St Katharine's and Holborn. In Southwark prostitution was tolerated under an elaborate code of restrictive conditions which attempted to limit its potential for nuisance while refusing to mitigate the evil of the trade as such. Prostitutes were to be protected by parish officers from beating or forcible detention or extortionate rents or entrapment into debt or being made to 'work' while sick or pregnant. On the other hand they were forbidden to wear the aprons which would have enabled them to pass as respectable women and were explicitly banned from honest by-employments like spinning. They were also obliged to quit the locality on holy days and when either parliament or the royal council was assembled. And when they died they were to be buried apart, in unconsecrated ground. Repeated fines show that these regulations were routinely disregarded.

The Southwark poll-tax returns of 1381 identified seven local 'stew-mongers', each of whom was fairly well-off, keeping between two and six servants, some of whom may actually have been servants. There were another dozen prostitutes, seemingly operating freelance from private lodgings, in the environs of St Thomas's Hospital. Others are known to have patrolled the soggy shrubberies of Paris Garden.

Local opinion hardened against prostitution over time and acted successfully by petitioning parliament to curb the extension of bordellos into the Guildable manor and other parts of the locality. House leases had clauses inserted, explicitly banning the use of premises for immoral purposes. In 1504, when there were eighteen stewhouses in operation, they were closed down by royal proclamation, prompted by a general fear of the spread of syphilis. The ban lasted just a year but only a dozen establishments reopened.

Although documented fines confirm that some women were forced into prostitution by kidnap, rape or deception, many seem to have been driven to it by simple economic need and the lack of alternative employment. Population pressure in the early sixteenth century seems to have worsened the situation, causing extensive female pauperisation, among widows and young immigrants especially. Their plight was exploited by keepers of the locality's numerous alehouses. Increasingly prostitution became associated in the public mind with shady characters, criminality and public disorder. Popular reaction against open bawdry created general support for a complete ban on brothels by royal proclamation in 1546. Deprived of regular employment the former bawds of Bankside appear to have dispersed rather than disappeared. In 1549 Bishop Latimer complained in a sermon preached before Edward VI "My Lords you have put down the stews: but I pray you what is the matter amended? ... Ye have but changed the place and not taken the whoredom away ... I here say there is now more whoredom in London than ever there was on the Bank."

Southwark continued to harbour prostitutes and barely disguised brothels. The latter are mentioned by Stow. Joan, wife of Edward Alleyn, was publicly 'carted' following allegations of involvement in brothel-keeping. The most noto-

rious and luxurious establishment was located in the old manor house of Paris Garden and was referred to in 1593 by the pamphleteer Thomas Nashe in *Christ's Teares over Jerusalem* in which he alleged that a dinner taken there alone cost £20. From December 1631 to January 1632 the establishment, then run by one Elizabeth Holland, was virtually besieged by the forces of law and order, an incident which won it the sobriquet of 'Holland's Leaguer'. The name Holland – real or assumed – implies a continuity with the tradition of recruiting prostitutes from the Low Countries. 'Leaguer' was the technical term for an armed camp of besiegers. Bess Holland's place was, apparently, protected by its own moat, drawbridge and portcullis and evidently had sufficient supplies to set the no doubt chilly besiegers at defiance. At any rate Bess appears to have successfully ignored two summonses to the Court of High Commission and re-established her business elsewhere. Ben Jonson's protégé, the wastrel Shackerley Marmion (1603-39), wrote a play about what seems to have struck even the

*39. Southwark Fair, from the engraving by Hogarth (1733).*

authorities as a rather farcical incident – *Holland's Leaguer. An excellent Comedy as it hath bin lately and often acted with great applause by the high and mighty Prince Charles his servants, at the Private House in Salisbury Court.* A prose work, also entitled *Holland's Leaguer,* appeared the same year, claiming to expose practices of sexual perversion.

## SOUTHWARK FAIR

Southwark Fair was formally established in the reign of Edward IV and was originally sanctioned to last three days, from the 7th to the 9th of September. Eventually it was to last an entire fortnight, expanding, in scale as well as duration, to block Borough High Street entirely, as well as spilling over into surrounding side streets. John Evelyn visited the fair in 1660 and saw monkeys dance and turn somersaults on a rope while holding candles, baskets of eggs and jugs of water. In 1668 Pepys saw a puppet show which told the story of Dick Whittington. He also bought wine for a famous tight-rope acrobat, Jacob Hall. Hogarth's famous depiction of the fair in 1733 included the best-known street-performers of the day - tumblers, conjurors, the 'German giant' and James Fig, the celebrated pugilist and fencer. Southwark Fair was finally suppressed in 1762.

## PARIS GARDEN

Paris Garden was opened to the public for bowling and gambling in the mid-sixteenth century by William Baiseley, Bailiff of Southwark. It remained in use as a recreational area for about a century but increasingly acquired an unsavoury reputation. Thomas Lupton, writing in 1632, was scathing about Paris Garden: "This may better bee termed a foule dene then a faire garden...Here come few that either regard their credit or losse of time; the swaggering Roarer, the cunning cheater, the rotten bard and the bloudy Butcher have their rendezvous here." By the time of the Commonwealth the area was being used for cloth-bleaching. It was built over for housing in the following decades.

## THE BEAR GARDENS

Bear-baiting as a royal spectacle dates back at least to 1484 when the office of Master of the Bears was instituted. In 1539 Henry VIII watched bears being baited at Paris Garden from the prudent security of a barge moored offshore.

The first documented mention of bear-baiting as a commercial entertainment in London dates from 1546 and refers specifically to Bankside as its location. There was also a small ring in St Margaret's Hill in the 1540s. A record of legal proceedings dated 1620 enumerates four other locations for bear-baiting. Excavations on the site of Benbow House revealed that old horses were butchered there to feed the mastiffs used for baiting. So were old or badly injured mastiffs themselves.

Elizabeth I thought bear-baiting a sufficiently appropriate entertainment for the French and Spanish ambassadors to view it but contemporary moralist Robert Crowley was contemptuous in his condemnation of onlookers:

> And yet every Sunday they will surely spend
> One penny or two the bearward's living to mend.
> At Paris Garden, each Sunday a man shall not fail
> To find two or three hundreds for the bearward's vail [profit].

Spectators themselves sometimes came to an end no more enviable than the luckless bears and dogs. In 1554 a blind bear broke loose and bit a man so severely that he died of his wounds. Like many Bankside buildings bear-baiting rings were flimsily-built fire-hazards. In January 1583 Lord Mayor Thomas Blank recorded with self righteous satisfaction that the collapse of scaffolding at Bankside during a bear-baiting had killed seven spectators outright and injured many more: "It giveth great occasion to acknowledge the hand of god for such abuse of the sabbath day." Sabbatarian preacher John Field estimated that a thousand people had been present when the mishap occurred. The proprietors swiftly rebuilt a larger and sturdier structure, which is illustrated on John Norden's map of 1593.

In 1604 Edward Alleyn, the foremost actor of the day, and his father-in-law, impresario Philip Henslowe jointly gained the lucrative appointment of Master Overseer and Ruler of the Bears, Bulls and Mastiff Dogs. One event was announced by poster as follows:

> "Tomorrow being Thursdaie shall be seen at the Bear-gardin on the bankside a greate mach plaid by the champins of Essex who hath chalenged all comers whatsoever to plaie v dogges at the single beare for V pounds and also to wearie a bull dead at the stake and for your better content shall have pleasant sport with the horse and ape and whiping of the blind beare"

Acting had made Alleyn and Henslowe rich.

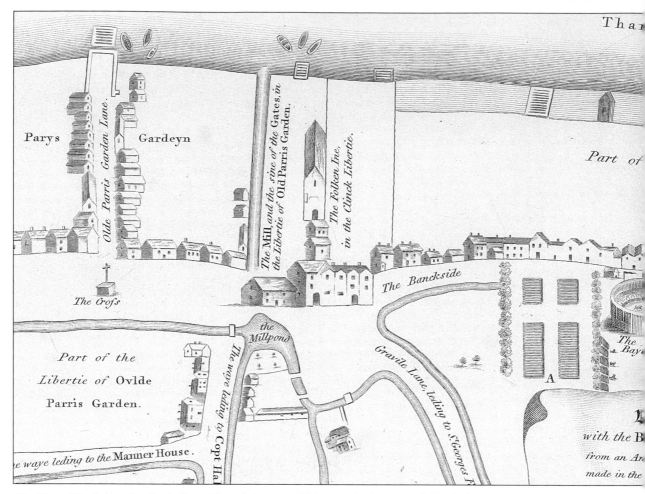

*40.  Plan of Bankside, showing bull- and bear-baiting establishments in the reign of Elizabeth I.*

Bear-baiting paid even better than plays and made them richer still. Henslowe's accounts for the Christmas period in 1608 show three days' takings at the Fortune theatre in Shoreditch to have been £5. 14. 9d while the same three days yielded £13. 13 .0d from the bear garden. Apart from the takings of shows they staged themselves they earned extra revenues from franchising other presenters, licensing itinerant bearwards, selling mastiffs, putting on shows at court and the Tower, as well as from profits made from betting on the outcome of each contest. The business was sufficiently profitable to justify a rebuilding of the Bear Pit in 1613, though the premises also doubled as the Hope Theatre. Shut for the plague in 1640 and shut down by the Puritans in 1642, the site was still marked as the scene of "Beere Bayting" in Hollar's 1647 panorama of London.

The premises were, however, pulled down in 1655 and the bears shot by a squad of soldiers.

Baiting was revived after the Restoration at a venue which became known as Davis's Amphitheatre. Pepys recorded in his diary for 14 August 1666 "After dinner I went with my wife and Mercer to the Bear Garden ... and saw some good sport of the bulls tossing the dogs into the very boxes. But it is a very rude, nasty pleasure." Pepys went back in May 1667 to watch a prize fight between a butcher and a waterman. When the waterman dropped his sword the butcher, who had been getting the better of the contest all along, slashed his opponent across the wrist "so as he was disabled to fight any longer". The watermen in the crowd judged this foul play and within minutes there was a free-for-all between them and the butchers looking on, who rallied

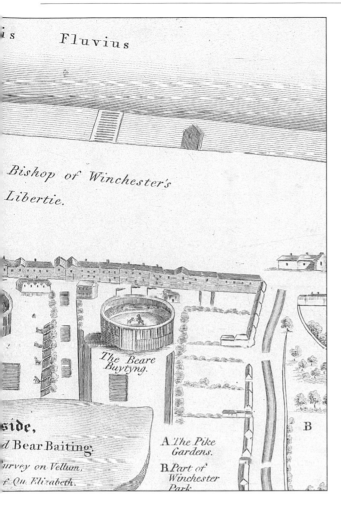

41. *Samuel Pepys, Secretary to the Admiralty.*

to defend their champion. Pepys recorded this additional free spectacle as "pleasant to see, but that I ... feared that in the tumult I might get some hurt." He nevertheless returned again in September 1667 and April 1669 to see more prize fights. Pepys's friend and fellow-diarist John Evelyn went in June 1670 "to the Beare Gardens, where was cock-fighting, dog-fighting, bear and bull baiting... Two poor dogs were killed and so all ended with the ape on horseback and I most heartily weary of the rude and dirty pastime." In 1676 bear-baiting was put on for the delectation of the Spanish ambassador. The last definite mention of a bull or bear ring is in 1682. During William III's reign the regular venue for baiting was transferred to Hockley-in-the-Hole in Clerkenwell as more convenient for the butchers of Smithfield who were its chief patrons.

## THE DOG AND DUCK

A Dog and Duck tavern stood in St George's Fields by 1642, testifying to the pursuit of wildfowling with spaniels on nearby ponds. The name is said to have come from the imagined shape of two of the three ponds. The earliest known advertisement for curative mineral waters dates from 1731, although the wells were being used as early as 1695. At fourpence a gallon the waters were touted "for the cure of rheumatism, stone, gravel, fistula, ulcers, cancers, sore eyes, and in all kinds of scorbutic cases whatever, and are remarkable for restoring a lost appetite.". Writing a century later William Rendle, speaking as much perhaps as a Medical Officer of Health as a local antiquary, expressed total scepticism that waters from such a noisome, marshy sinkhole as St George's Fields could have any medicinal value whatsoever, opining rather that the 'spring' represented no more than diverted ditchwater. In 1769 the attractions of the 'spa' were enhanced by the addition of tea-rooms, a swimming bath, skittles and a bowling green. Dr Johnson recommended the waters to Mrs Thrale in 1771. A different note was struck in 1774 in the prologue to soldier-dramatist John Burgoyne's rustic comedy The Maid of the Oaks:

St George's Fields, with taste and fashion struck
Display Arcadia at the Dog and Duck.

42.  *The Bear Garden on Bankside.*

43.  *Bear baiting in the early nineteenth century, by H.Alken.*

44. *Cuper's Gardens. Its site is now covered by the southern approach to Waterloo Bridge.*

And Drury Misses here, in tawdry pride,
Are there 'Pastoras' by the fountain side;
To frowsy bowers they reel through midnight
    damps,
With Fawns half drunk, and Dryads breaking
    lamps.

The spa finally went out of business in 1799 and the Bethlem Royal Hospital was subsequently built over its site in 1811-15 (*see p71*). Profits from the Dog and Duck were used by the Hedger family, its proprietors, to finance the building of West Square.

## CUPER'S GARDENS

Cuper's Gardens – perhaps inevitably more popularly known as Cupid's Gardens – stood on three acres of land leased from the Earl of Arundel by his gardener, Abraham Boydell Cuper. An adjoining seven acres, leased from the Archbishop of Canterbury, were added in 1686. Rocque's map of 1746 shows a river-front landing stage, Cuper's Stairs or Cuper's Bridge, which implies a steady trade from the City side. Until 1720 it had been the mooring-place of a floating pleasure palace with the appropriate name of Folly. Folly had an upper, open deck with turrets and an enclosed lower deck with curtained booths. Pepys recorded visiting it in April 1668. Queen Mary II's fondness for it won it the sobriquet of 'the Royal Diversion' and implies a certain level of respectability, but this had quite disappeared by 1710, when it was visited by the German traveller Z.C. von Uffenbach, who was as shocked by prices that were "prodigious dear" as much as by the "innumerable harlots" plying their trade there. This impression of social decline is confirmed by the Prologue to *Mrs. Centilivre's Busy Body* of 1708:

The Fleet-Street sempstress, toast of Temple
    sparks
That runs spruce neckcloths for attorneys'
    clerks
At Cupid's gardens will her hours regale,
Sing 'fair Dorinda' and drink bottled ale.

Long and narrow in shape, Cuper's Gardens were laid out with winding paths among trees and shrubbery, punctuated with busts and statues plundered from Arundel House in the Strand at the time of its demolition. A lake was created on the west side; there were bowling greens and an adjacent tavern, The Feathers, supplied refreshments. Entrance at a shilling kept out the riff-raff. After Ephraim Evans took over in 1738 evening concerts were given. A ban on liveried servants was enforced and watchmen appointed to ward off footpads tempted to prey on patrons approaching via St George's Fields. Evans died in 1740 but his widow, appropriately known to all as 'The Widow', kept up the standard of the entertainments, adding elaborate firework displays to attract an up-market clientele, including the Prince of Wales himself. Despite this, the establishment's licence was revoked after the passage of the 1753 'Act for the Better Preventing of Thefts and Robberies and for Regulating Places of Public Entertainment'. Cuper's Gardens remained open as a venue for tea and continued to provide concerts and fireworks for subscribers until 1760. In 1762 a vinegar distillery was built on the site. That was demolished when the approaches to Waterloo Bridge were being laid out.

## FINCH'S GROTTO GARDENS

The closure of Cuper's Gardens appears to have inspired the opening of this attraction in 1760 on a triangular plot near St George's Road, where a grotto was built over a medicinal spring at the expense of Thomas Finch, an heraldic painter. An octagonal music-room occupied by an orchestra and guest stars from Covent Garden and Sadler's Wells gave added tone. Fireworks were introduced in 1771 but failed to turn around what was evidently a failing business. The grotto was demolished in 1773 to make way for a skittle ground, the Goldsmith's Tavern and a workhouse for the parish of St Saviour.

## RESTORATION SPRING GARDENS

The appropriately named Restoration Tavern dated from the early years of the reign of Charles II. An advertisement of 1714 confirms it as a venue for cock-fighting but by 1733 a new source of income was being secured to its proprietors through the exploitation of a spring whose waters

*45. Finch's Grotto, near St George's Road.*

46. *The Surrey Theatre, 1812.*

were deemed efficacious for the treatment of "all cancerous and scorbutic humors". Shortly afterwards a second, chalybeate spring was discovered. The water from this spring was sufficiently valued to be made available for sale at Exeter Change in the Strand. Botanist William Curtis (1746-99), author of *Flora Londoniensis,* took over the site in the 1770s and laid out a botanical garden, open to subscribers, before removing it to a new site in Brompton in 1789.

## THE SURREY THEATRE

When it opened in 1782 on a piece of ground on the west side of Blackfriars Road this venue was called the Royal Circus and Equestrian Philharmonic Academy, but its grandiose name offered no guarantee of success or protection against disaster. The lessor was local landowner Col. Temple West and the lessees were Charles Hughes, a trick horse rider, who had been at Astley's famous establishment, and the song-writer and showman Charles Dibdin (1745-1814). Unfortunately, Dibdin had rather a gift for making enemies, who came to include Hughes. The joint venture ended in debt and recrimination, though after an abortive flight to India which got as far as Torbay, Dibdin did settle for a while in St George's Fields.

The Royal Circus then burned down but was rebuilt. Drunken, eccentric actor-manager Robert Elliston (1774-1831) became the proprietor in 1809 and blatantly evaded the Patent Act (which strictly limited the number of theatres which could produce plays) by the crude but effective ploy of simply inserting a ballet into every play – including *Hamlet* and *Macbeth.* Elliston moved on in 1814. In 1816 the name Surrey Theatre was adopted as the management passed to one of Charles Dibdin's numerous illegitimate brood, Thomas (1771-1841), who proved as quarrelsome and disaster-prone as his sire. Thomas Dibdin lived at 143 Blackfriars Road from 1817 to 1820. The venture bankrupted him and he was forced to close in 1822. The theatre then reverted once more to down-market entertainments, such as circus, until Elliston, having been bankrupted by managing Drury Lane and ruined in health by two seizures, returned in 1827 and thanks to Douglas Jerrold's *Black-Eyed Susan* finally brought off a box-office triumph in 1829. Elliston's efforts to continue on stage shattered his precarious constitution and, following a third seizure, he died at his home in Great Surrey Street in July 1831. Hailed by Byron, Macready, Mathews and Leigh Hunt as a talent second only to Garrick, Elliston was intermittently a great man of the theatre brought low by petty weaknesses. Another period of relative success at the Surrey, from 1848 to 1869, was achieved, despite another fire and swift rebuilding in 1865, by the partnership of Dick Shepherd, pioneering producer of unsophisticated melodrama, and William Creswick (1813-88), his lead actor and a ham of the old school.

*47.  George Conquest (1837-1901), actor-manager of the Surrey Theatre, 1895.*

In 1881 the Surrey's fortunes revived again when its proprietorship passed to George Conquest (1837-1901), another melodrama man, who put on lavish pantomimes every Christmas. Trained as an 'acrobatic pantomimist', Conquest claimed to have put on forty-five productions and appeared in twenty-seven of them. He also wrote or adapted over a hundred plays, claimed to have broken every bone in his face and body in the course of his career and is said to have invented the illusion of 'flying' by means of 'invisible' wires. Offstage he suffered from a speech impediment which disappeared completely when he was acting, one of his specialities being animal imitations. Unlike many of his profession, Conquest died a wealthy man, leaving a fortune of £64,000, which would put him in the millionaire bracket in modern terms. After Conquest's death the Surrey declined again, was briefly a cinema from 1920 to 1924, and was finally pulled down in 1934 after the Royal Ophthalmic Hospital bought its site to build an extension to its premises.

*48.  St George's Circus and Surrey Theatre. Drawing by Arthur Moreland.*

# Doing Good

## PAROCHIAL CHARITIES

The dissolution of the monasteries meant the destruction of a welfare system. The new Protestant morality urged the godly to regard their assets as goods held in stewardship, for whose use they would be accountable at the last. Pious benefactions therefore proliferated throughout the centuries, usually prompted by fore-shadowings of eternity. Most took the form of properties or, later, investments from which the income was to be disbursed at the discretion of trustees drawn from the ranks of the propertied and locally prominent. Some legacies were for substantial ventures, such as schools or almshouses, but many were intended to meet the immediate and pressing needs of the indigent. Emerson's bequest of 1620 and Buckland's of 1628 provided for coals and small sums of cash. Elizabeth Newcomen's of 1675 provided clothes for poor children. A century later, in 1780, John Stock left money to clothe poor women.

## HOUSING

Charitable impulses stretching over several centuries supplied some of the local need for decent accommodation. Cure's College almshouses were erected in Deadman's Place (Park Street) in 1584. Thomas Cure served Edward VI, Mary and Elizabeth as Master of the Horse and also represented Southwark in Parliament. In 1579 he bought Waverley House from Viscount Montague and in 1584 obtained letters patent to establish a college or hospital. Cure's College included six existing almshouses built by St Saviour's and was subsequently enriched by further endowments. The College moved out in 1863.

The Fishmongers' almshouses were built at the corner of St George's Road and Newington Butts in 1618, with their own garden and chapel. Further accommodation was added adjacent in 1719. They survived until 1851.

In 1717 Edward Edwards, a parishioner of Christ Church, executed a deed of gift, assigning lands to trustees to be used after his death for charitable purposes. These were to include the endowment of the charity school, a Christmas Day distribution of beef and beer and the purchase of land

*49. Cure's College, Park Street, before 1862, when the almshouses were demolished*

*50. Drapers' Almshouses, 1851.*

*52. Alleyn's Almshouses, from a sketch dated 1840.*

for almshouses. In 1752 a piece of land called the Physic Garden, to the south of Green Walk (now Burrell Street), was bought and over forty almshouses built there. Houses were also put up in nearby streets to provide a continuing revenue for the scheme. The Burrell Street almshouses were rebuilt in 1895.

The Drapers' almshouses were the gift, anonymous in his lifetime, of John Walter, Clerk to the Company. Initially they consisted of just two houses with four rooms in each, to accommodate no less than sixteen inmates. They were relocated and rebuilt in the eighteenth century and again in 1819-20 in Glasshill Street.

*51. Peabody Square, Blackfriars Road.*

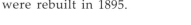

Hopton's almshouses were erected in 1752 from the bequest of Charles Hopton, a fishmonger who died childless in 1731 and appears never to have lived in Southwark, although he did own lands in Christ Church parish. The enactment of his bequest was delayed by its diversion to the benefit of his sister Elizabeth until her death in 1739. In 1743 land was bought "near the Green walk" and the existing buildings torn down. They were replaced by twenty-six, from 1825 twenty-eight almshouses and a pine panelled committee room.

Overman's almshouses were established by Alice Overman in 1771. Almshouses were also established in honour of the Revd Rowland Hill (*see p87*).

A more modern approach to counteract the sort of slums portrayed in *The Builder* (*see ills. 53 & 54*) was represented by the construction of the various Peabody Estates, part of a London wide initiative funded by the philanthropic trust established by American banker George Peabody (1795-1862) to provide well-made, strictly managed accommodation to enable the respectable working poor to remain just that, rather than sliding into the underclass which so often surrounded and overwhelmed them. Blocks built by the Improved Industrial Dwellings Company represent one of many imitators of the Peabody scheme. Born to wealth and comfort, Octavia Hill

54. *Ewer Street, Gravel Lane.*

53. *Duke Street, today known as Duke Street Hill, Tooley Street.*

(1838-1912) came under the Christian Socialist influence of F.D. Maurice and, with the advice of John Ruskin, devoted herself to the management of housing for the poor, starting on a small scale in her own neighbourhood, Marylebone. Her approach was methodical rather than visionary and she attached as much importance to refurbishing existing housing stock as to providing new dwellings. In 1884 the Ecclesiastical Commissioners placed in her hands their extensive property portfolio in Southwark – Redcross Cottages, Whitecross Cottages and Gable Cottages were among her creations. Apart from her widely influential efforts in tackling London's housing problem, Octavia Hill was also responsible for founding the Charity Organisation Society and the National Trust. The memorial service organised to honour her life of charitable devotion was held in Southwark Cathedral.

## MAGDALEN HOSPITAL

England's first reformatory for penitent prostitutes was initially established in Whitechapel in 1758. Its creators were Robert Dingley (1710-81), a Russia merchant, director of the Bank of England, dilettante (FSA, ERS) and expert collector of gem stones, and his former business partner

*55. Revd William Dodd, 1729-1777.*

and fellow governor of the Foundling Hospital Jonas Hanway (1712-86), who became celebrated for his philanthropy, his virulent opposition to tea-drinking and his pioneering use of the umbrella. They may well have counted themselves fortunate to have the inaugural sermon preached by William Dodd (1729-77), a veritable star of the pulpit, who specialised in pleading the cause of charities. Dodd was subsequently appointed chaplain to the Magdalen. From 1763 onwards he was voted a salary of £100 a year and meanwhile began to develop a subsidiary income as an author of edifying volumes.

The Magdalen project proved so successful that within a decade it proved necessary to look for larger premises. These were erected at St George's Fields between 1769 and 1772, largely to the designs of Dingley himself, a gifted amateur architect. Thanks to the patronage of the great and extraordinary strokes of fortune for his wife – an inheritance of £1,500 and a lottery win of another £1,000 – Dodd's star meanwhile rose ever higher. Tutor to Lord Chesterfield's son, with a proprietary chapel in Pimlico and a country house in Ealing, Dodd became a darling of London society – and began to run up debts. An attempt to bribe his way into the prosperous and fashionable living of St George's, Hanover Square, backfired, obliging him to visit his former pupil in Switzerland while the heat died down. Returning to London, he was still highly regarded enough to have his portrait placed in the board-room of the new Magdalen Hospital. Debt, however, soon overwhelmed him and in August 1774, he lost his chaplaincy at the hospital. Dodd sold off his Pimlico chapel to raise cash and then in 1777 forged a bond in the name of Lord Chesterfield. The forgery was uncovered and, despite the strenuous efforts of Dr Johnson to avert the worst, Dodd was sent to the gallows.

The Magdalen Hospital removed to Streatham in 1868 and later became an 'approved school' for young offenders.

## SCHOOL FOR THE INDIGENT BLIND

This institution, the first of its kind in London, was established in 1800 thanks to the efforts of Shute Barrington, Bishop of Durham, businessman Sir Thomas Bernard and James Ware, a specialist of ophthalmic surgery at St Thomas's. Its first premises were a room in the former Dog and Duck tavern (*see p47*), capable of accommodating an initial fifteen pupils. Soon the whole building was taken over as the number of pupils rose to over fifty. In 1811-12 purpose-built accommodation – "more commendable for utility than for its beauty"– was erected. As numbers rose past the hundred mark in the 1830s the School's buildings were extended to designs by local architect John Newman (*see p110*). The 'core curriculum' consisted of practical skills, such as knitting and making mats and baskets, which would enable students to gain a useful livelihood. But broader concerns were not entirely overlooked: W.H.Monk became the School's professor of music. He is best remembered as the musical editor of *Hymns Ancient and Modern* and for his composition *Abide with me*. The School moved out to new premises in Leatherhead in 1901.

## THE ROYAL FREEMASONS' CHARITY SCHOOL FOR FEMALE CHILDREN

Founded in 1788 and initially located on the north side of Westminster Bridge Road, this school took up to a hundred girls aged between five and ten. Recruits were required to be the daughters of freemasons of at least three years' standing, to have had the smallpox and to be free of any defect or infirmity. The curriculum, such as it was, concentrated on domestic skills and aimed "to impress strongly on their minds a due sense of subordination, in true humility and obedience to their superiors". Girls were discharged into domestic service or apprenticeships at fifteen. The school relocated to Wandsworth in 1852.

## THE PHILANTHROPIC SOCIETY

This school was founded in 1778 for child criminals and the "offspring of convicted felons". By 1793 it was equipped with not only classrooms and dormitories but also a chapel and workshops. The project was funded partly by collections taken up from the congregation attending the chapel and partly from the sale of work produced by the inmates. Boys were set to master trades well represented in the Southwark area– printing, book-binding, tailoring, shoemaking and the manufacture of rope and twine; girls were set to domestic tasks, such as washing and mending, and also made clothes for themselves and the boys. By the 1840s financial difficulties obliged the school to limit its intake to boys. At the end of the decade the institution moved out to Redhill so that the boys could be set to agricultural work. The site of the former school was later occupied by Notre Dame High School.

*56. The Freemasons' Charity School in St George's Fields.*

57. *The Benevolent Society of St Patrick in Stamford Street. It was founded in 1784.*

## CHILDREN'S HOMES

Charlotte Sharman began finding rural foster-homes for Southwark orphans in 1862. In 1867 she set up an orphanage in a house (later two) in West Square and also developed an adoption agency. Purpose-built accommodation was then built in Astral (then South) Street between 1875 and 1884. In 1882 J.W.C. Fegan, another compassionate crusader, opened a children's home in Southwark Street, which survived until its lease ran out in 1913.

## THE GRAMMAR SCHOOLS

In 1562 Letters Patent were granted by the Crown for the establishment of a school to educate up to a hundred scholars from the new parish of St Saviour's. The subsequent establishment of two scholarships to maintain alumni at university shows that the brightest, at least, were expected to achieve more than was needed for a merely local career. Latin poet Christopher Ocland (?died 1590) was appointed master in 1572, though his erudition did him little good and he eventually died in dire poverty. The school was initially housed in part of the Green Dragon, formerly Cobham's Inn. It was supported financially by rents from the former chapel of St Margaret's church (*see p99*) and later by revenues from the Three Tuns, the Red Lyon and blocks of tenements behind the Queen's Head and in Kent (now Tabard) Street. The fire of 1676 necessitated rehousing the school in purpose-built premises. In 1838 it moved to a cramped location on the north side of Sumner Street where it eventually became hedged in and overshadowed by high buildings. By the late Victorian period its enrolment had dwindled to just twenty-three pupils and in 1899 it finally amalgamated with St Olave's Grammar School. St Saviour's alumni include the distinguished teacher of medicine William Heberden (1710-1801), Lord Mayor, philanthropist and printer Sir Sydney Waterlow (1822-1906) and reforming High Master of St Paul's school, F.E.W. Walker (1830-1910).

St Olave's Grammar School was established in 1571. Unlike St Saviour's it expanded in the nineteenth century and in 1896 took the initiative in bringing about a merger of the two establishments and founding a separate new school for girls, which opened in the New Kent Road in

1903. Distinguished alumni of St.Olave's include pioneering medievalist T.F.Tout (1855-1929), botanist Alfred Barton Rendle (1865-1938) and Sir William Ashley (1860-1927) for whom Harvard created the first professorial chair in economic history in the English-speaking world. Sir Leon Bagrit (1902-79), son of Russian immigrants, entered St Olave's unable to speak English but went on to win a prize for English literature and show promise as a violinist. Despite reading law, he made his career in engineering to become a leading exponent of automation, the subject of his 1966 Reith Lectures.

*58. Sir Sydney Waterlow, Lord Mayor of London and former pupil of St Saviour's Grammar School*

*59. St Saviour's Free Grammar School (publ.1815).*

60.  *St Olave's Grammar School in Tooley Street (publ. 1813).*

61.  *St Olave's School, 1836.*

## OTHER ESTABLISHMENTS

Elizabeth Newcomen established a charity school in her name in 1675. St Saviour's parish school was founded thanks to the generosity of Mrs Dorothy Applebee and initially located in St Saviour's churchyard. It subsequently moved to Union Street to share premises for a while with the Newcomen school and from there it moved in 1977 to Redcross Way. It is now known as the Cathedral School of St Saviour and St Mary Overie. St George the Martyr parish school was established in 1698. It subsequently amalgamated with St Jude's, Colnbrook Street. Christ Church established a parochial school for boys in 1713 and another for girls in 1719. The London Nautical School in Stamford Street was housed in buildings originally erected in 1803 for the education of the children of the local Irish community.

In 1830 King Edward's School, founded in the City in 1553, moved to St George's Fields, occupying a site between West Square and the Bethlem Hospital. Initially more of a reformatory than a school as such it became exclusively educational from 1850 onwards, preparing boys mainly for the navy and girls for domestic service. The boys' department moved out to Surrey in 1867 and the girls' closed down in 1922.

As with churches the Southwark area proved to be under-resourced with schools as its population expanded in the second half of the nineteenth century. From the 1870s onwards the London School Board began to make good the deficiency, erecting some seven schools in north Southwark alone, thus providing places for some five thousand pupils. As a result some church schools began to contract or close altogether. Webber Street school is now the Jerwood Arts Centre.

## PRIVATE ENTERPRISE

Edward Cocker (1631-75), teacher of penmanship and arithmetic, originally worked in the area of St Paul's as a 'scrivener and engraver' and by the age of thirty was eminent enough to receive a gift of £150 from Charles II, a monarch more noted for promising bounties than actually providing them. Pepys described Cocker as "very ingenious and well read in all our English poets" and shared with him a passion for collecting books and manuscripts. Cocker subsequently established a school near St George the Martyr, Southwark but died at forty-one, a contemporary squib attributing his fate to brandy. Cocker was buried at St George's, as near as possible to his former school. After his death the school was taken over by his friend and former assistant John Hawkins, who was also to be buried at St George's. Cocker is credited with producing over thirty texts, with titles such as *The Pen's Gallantry, The Young Lawyer's Writing Master* and *Cocker's Compleat Arithmetician. Cocker's Arithmetic,* published posthumously under the guidance of Hawkins and with a preface by a Fellow of the Royal Society, ran to over a hundred editions, including special versions for Scotland and Ireland. Half a century after Cocker's death the author of a guide-book to London could still deem it appropriate to insert notice in it of the last resting-place of "the famous Cocker".

Presbyterian divine Joshua Oldfield (1656-1729) established an academy for training dissenting ministers at Coventry and brought it with him when he became minister to a congregation meeting at Globe Alley, Maid Lane. The academy appears to have been highly respected among dissenters and Oldfield himself was likewise esteemed by Locke and Newton, whom he numbered among his personal acquaintance.

Thomas Crosby (died after 1749) kept a mathematical and commercial school at Horselydown and wrote a textbook *The Book-Keeper's Guide* but is chiefly remembered for his four volume *History of the English Baptists from the Reformation to the beginning of the reign of George I.* Its value to subsequent historians was substantially vitiated by the author's failure to distinguish with any precision just what exactly constituted a Baptist.

## A FAILED REVOLUTIONARY

Joseph Lancaster (1778-1838) was born in Southwark, the son of a shopkeeper who had fought as a soldier in the American War of Independence. A youth of strong, if unfocused, religious feeling, Lancaster ran away from home with the idea of going to the West Indies to teach the poor slaves about Jesus, got as far as Bristol, enlisted in the Royal Navy because he had no money and was fortunate to be released from his engagement after a single voyage. Returning home to Southwark, Lancaster became a Quaker and began to bring local 'street arabs' home to instruct them in the rudiments of literacy. Discovering a gift for teaching and a natural classroom authority, he opened a school in the Borough Road in 1801. Above it he placed a sign – "All who will may send their children and have them educated freely and those who do not wish to have education for nothing may pay for it if they please." On these

62. *Joseph Lancaster, 1778-1838, a pioneer in the movement to establish a national education system.*

kingdom should be able to read the Bible for himself. Lancaster, by virtue of this single encounter, had become a national figure. In 1806 the children's author Laetitia Barbauld wrote admiringly from Stoke Newington:

> Upon sending for the Account you have published of your excellent school, I find it is not to be had of the Booksellers, but only of yourself. Can you put us in a way to get it? ... Permit me to take this occasion of expressing the very great pleasure experienced by Mr Barbauld and myself, when we lately visited your school, and saw with our own eyes the effect of your admirable method. We were unfortunate indeed in one circumstance, the not finding you there, and not being able to pay you those acknowledgements to which, as one of the Benefactors of mankind you have so just a claim.

It was at this point of widespread acclaim that things began to go wrong. Lancaster's school was attacked by Anglican traditionalists for being outside the control of the established Church. Given that Britain had been at war with revolutionary France for over a decade anything that might stir the ambitions of the lower social orders could be made to seem threatening to a nation still seemingly in peril. Lancaster's personal circumstances complicated matters further as sympathisers had to rally round to pay off his debts. Controversy continued to mount. Supporters of what from 1808 was called the Royal Lancasterian Society, no less, included most leading dissenters and heavyweight intellectuals like Henry Brougham and the favoured organ of their network, the *Edinburgh Review*. Ranged against them were virtually the entire Anglican clergy and the *Quarterly Review*, which championed a rival cause, the National Society, which was to be founded in 1811. Sneeringly dismissive of Lancaster's pedagogy, his critics credited Bell with originating whatever virtues it might have. Lancaster and Bell declined to engage personally in the fray and remained on warm personal terms, Lancaster never denying his debt to his mentor and concentrating his energies on a punishing propaganda mission. He reported to his supporters that in the year 1809-10 he had travelled 3,775 miles, given 67 public lectures to 23,480 hearers, helped establish fifty Lancasterian schools for 14,200 pupils and raised £3,850 for the movement. By then there were similar establishments in New York, Philadelphia and Boston and in 1810 a delegation, including 'the Liberator', Simon Bolivar himself, came all the way from newly-

quixotically generous terms enrolment expanded quickly from ninety to five hundred and Lancaster was soon obliged to employ the 'Madras system' originated by Alexander Bell in India, whereby senior pupils acted as mentors to junior ones, passing on what they had learned from the teacher himself. With a thousand pupils on the books, Lancaster's experiment soon attracted the notice of the philanthropically-minded dukes of Bedford and Sussex. Lancaster was sufficiently encouraged in 1803 to publish his first pamphlet *Improvements in Education*. Despite its apparent success the Borough Road establishment was, from sheer economic necessity, conducted with the utmost frugality. Spelling books were cut up and the pages pasted onto boards to be passed around. Younger children learned to shape their letters using their fingers and a sand-table. Discipline was maintained by a complex system of carrots and sticks - ranks, titles and badges for the obedient and enthusiastic, punishments ranging from being tied to a pillar to being confined to a cage for the disruptive and recalcitrant. In 1805 Lancaster was summoned to Weymouth for an audience of the king himself. George III pledged to become a subscriber to the school and expressed the hope that one day every child in his

63. *A classroom in a Lancaster school, showing the monitorial system in action.*

independent Venezuela to inspect and admire Lancaster's self-proclaimed revolution in education.

Lancaster himself, however, chafed at growing institutional restraint. The price of having his debts paid off was to become answerable to a committee of management. When Lancaster finally broke free to found his own establishment at Tooting it quickly went bankrupt. Meanwhile in 1812 the Borough Road institution and its imitators metamorphosed into the British and Foreign Schools Society, an enduring rival in the dissenting cause to the Anglican National Society. These two competing organisations would become the main providers of elementary education in Britain until the advent of Board Schools from 1870 onwards. In 1816 the British and Foreign Schools Society established a teacher training college, which survived until 1888 and in 1892 metamorphosed into the Borough Road Polytechnic Institute, now South Bank University.

Lancaster emigrated in 1818 to try his luck in Baltimore, then Caracas and finally Montreal. All his ventures failed as he became increasingly embittered until he died in New York as a result of a street accident. In perspective it is clear that Lancaster's pupil-teacher system represented at best a false start in mass education. Practical experience of its severe limitations soon confirmed that there could be no short cut round the provision of adequate numbers of properly trained teachers. But Lancaster had made mass education for the poor a question of public policy and had personally aroused in thousands of impoverished but ambitious children the desire to learn – no

bad epitaph for a man whose closing years were so sadly overshadowed by oppressive emotions of failure and betrayal.

Given its reliance on pupil-teachers it was wholly appropriate that Borough Road School should become Borough Road Training College and that many of its alumni should become distinguished educationalists. James Bonwick (1817-1906) went from teaching to writing as a pioneer of early Australian history. Sir Joshua Girling Fitch (1824-1903) became Principal of Borough Road and helped establish Girton College and the Girls' Public Day School Trust. T.J. Macnamara (1861-1931) became President of the National Union of Teachers and MP for North Camberwell. George Sampson (1873-1950) wrote the influential *English for the English* (1921) and was a friend of H.G. Wells and Arnold Bennett.

## THE SURREY INSTITUTION

The Surrey Institution was built in 1778-9 as The Rotunda to house the natural history collection of Sir Ashton Lever which had previously been on show at Leicester House and included items collected by Captain Cook on his voyages. The venture eventually failed and the collection was auctioned off piecemeal in 1806. The building was meanwhile reincarnated as The Surrey Institution, enthusiastically described in a contemporary guide book, produced by Ackermann the art publisher, as an "academic mansion", with a galleried and tiered lecture theatre capable of accommodating an audience of five hundred, plus a library and rooms for meetings, reading, conversation and the storage of large items of

64.  *Interior of the Surrey Institution, by Pugin and Rowlandson, 1809.*

'philosophical apparatus'. The library overlooked a garden "to convey an idea of rural retirement". The first lecture programme, in 1803, was biased towards the sciences and featured the German Friedrich Accum (1769-1838), who lectured on chemistry and mineralogy. These lectures became sufficiently well known to justify illustration by Rowlandson. Accum was later to join forces with Ackermann in promoting gas lighting in London. The Surrey Institution was later to sponsor Coleridge's celebrated lectures on Shakespeare and Hazlitt's discourses on the Comic Writers of England.

After an interlude as a theatre, the building was taken by the freethinker Richard Carlile (1790-1843), who had served eighteen weeks in King's Bench and then six years in Dorchester gaol for publishing subversive literature. Coinciding with a revolution in France and widespread agitation for the extension of the franchise in Britain,

Carlile's tenure of the Rotunda represented a brief but significant interlude in the struggle to establish freedom of political expression in speech and print. The Rotunda simultaneously served as the headquarters of the short-lived National Union of the Working Classes, one of several over-ambitious attempts to create a proto-revolutionary organisation transcending craft-based associations to advance proletarian rights. At his death Carlile bequeathed his body to St Thomas's hospital for dissection.

Two other temporary tenants of the Rotunda also tested the limits of freedom of opinion. Robert Taylor (1784-1844), a former pupil of Sir Astley Cooper (*see p69*), having foresworn the ward for the pulpit, drifted towards deism before being forced into the King's Bench prison by debt. An associate of Carlile, in May 1830 Taylor, dressed as a bishop, preached in the Rotunda and in consequence found himself dubbed 'the Devil's

65. *Emma Cons, founder of the Royal Victoria Hall in 1880, which later became the Old Vic Theatre. She also founded Morley College.*

Chaplain' and put on trial for blasphemy. After serving two years in Horsemonger Lane gaol, he married a wealthy older woman and decamped to France where he returned to the trade of surgery.

The spiritual career of Irish mystic John 'Zion' Ward (1781-1837) included phases of allegiance to the Baptists, Methodists, Independents, Sandemanians and Joanna Southcott, whose cause he attempted to perpetuate by proclaiming himself the second Messiah – Shiloh – she had promised to give birth to. Ward's preaching at the Rotunda in 1831 had no custodial consequences.

The Rotunda was eventually given over to commercial use and badly damaged by bombing in World War Two, The first edition of Pevsner (1952) suggested its restoration to create a museum dedicated to Southwark or Shakespeare. Judged past salvation, however, it was subsequently demolished in 1958.

## MORLEY COLLEGE

The College originated in an initiative of Emma Cons (1838-1912), owner of the Old Vic, and the first regular evening classes were given in the theatre dressing rooms in 1885. Miss Cons, a friend of Octavia Hill (*see p55*) and disciple of Ruskin, herself lived in a housing settlement of her own foundation at the junction of Lambeth and Kennington Roads, and exhausted herself in a wide range of causes, from temperance and suffragism to horticulture and careers guidance. In 1889 the institution was formalised as Morley College in honour of a supportive millionaire MP, Samuel Morley (1809-86). Its principals have included Eva Hubback (1886-1949), founder of the Townswomen's Guild and the redoubtable Barbara, later Baroness, Wootton (1897-1988). Composer Gustav Holst (1874-1934) joined the staff in 1907 and developed a highly successful annual music festival, staged at Thaxted in Essex. Later Sir Michael Tippett taught there. Designer Eric Ravilious (1903-42) painted a celebrated mural at the College, regrettably destroyed in World War Two.

# Hospitals and Healers

66. *St Thomas's Hospital, 1840.*

## ST THOMAS'S HOSPITAL

St Thomas's originated as part of the Priory of St Mary Overie, though it cannot have acquired its specific dedication until after the death of Thomas Becket in 1170. After the Priory was devastated by fire in the early thirteenth century the hospital was reconstructed on a new site on the east side of Borough High Street. The celebrated Dick Whittington donated a ward where unmarried mothers could give birth in discreet privacy. In 1535 the institution was condemned by Thomas Cromwell as "the bawdy hospital of S. Thomas in Southwark". Closed in 1540, it was reopened in 1551, when Edward VI granted the buildings to the Lord Mayor and citizens of London. Theological tact decreed a slight shift of designation and the Hospital of St Thomas the Martyr was reborn as the Hospital of St Thomas the Apostle. Whether or not Cromwell's gibe still stung a quarter of a century later, in 1561, it was decreed that unmarried pregnant women would be refused admission to an institution dedicated to "honest persons and not of harlottes". St Thomas's was substantially rebuilt between 1693 and 1709 through the generosity of Sir Robert Clayton, a former Lord Mayor. Regulations issued in 1700 banned the admission of persons deemed incurable or with infectious diseases. In 1703 the hospital acquired the services of Dr Richard Mead (1673-1754), who was to become the most distinguished practitioner of his day. A brilliant classicist, Mead had trained at two of Europe's most outstanding medical schools, Leyden and Padua, but had initially begun his practice in the house in which he had been born in Stepney. Mead gained instant celebrity with a treatise on poisons, based on his own daring experiment of swallowing viper's venom to prove that a puncture of the skin was necessary for it to produce fatal results. As a result Mead was elected FRS in the same year as he came to St Thomas's. By 1715 his practice had become so extensive that he exchanged his position at the hospital from that of employee to that of Governor. Mead's patients included Pope, Newton, Walpole, Queen Anne and the Princess of Wales. His single most influential act was to promote inoculation against smallpox, himself inoculating the royal family – after proving the harmless-

67. *St Thomas's Church and entrance to St Thomas's Hospital.*

68  *Dr Richard Mead, oil attributed to Allan Ramsay.*

ness of the procedure by experimenting on half a dozen criminals condemned to the gallows. Throughout his long life Mead retained his early interest in the classics and was respected as a distinguished antiquarian in his own right. An enthusiastic and discriminating bibliophile, he left a library of over ten thousand volumes. Mead's eminence is testified by the fact that he was sculpted by Roubiliac and memorialised in paint by Dahl and Ramsay. Dr Johnson's handsome epitaph was that "dr. mead lived more in the broad sunshine of life than almost any man."

Mead's career and character contrast strongly with that of 'Chevalier' John Taylor (1703-72), a St Thomas's man, who became a high-profile itinerant specialist operating for cataract. His detractors blame him for contributing to the blindness of both Bach and Handel.

The international career of Thomas Dimsdale (1712-1800) was, by contrast, unblemished by detraction. Having written the standard work on inoculation against smallpox, Dimsdale was summoned to Russia by Catherine the Great to inoculate both her and her heir. While the Empress had complete faith in her English consultant she feared that her people might not have and arranged for relays of fresh horses to be on standby for his escape should the enterprise miscarry. As it triumphed Dimsdale was rewarded with a Russian barony, £10,000 plus £2,000 for expenses, miniatures of the empress and her son set in diamond-studded frames and a pension of £500 for life.

Yorkshire Quaker John Fothergill (1712-80) established his reputation with *An Account of the Sore Throat*, which gave an accurate clinical account of diphtheria based on his own experiences during the London epidemic of 1747-8. Fothergill built up a lucrative London practice and, largely barred from official appointments by his Quakerism, had the time as well as the money to establish a superb botanical garden at Upton, near Stratford. Sir Joseph Banks thought that it was only equalled by Kew itself. Fothergill also built up major collections of shells and insects and employed a team of artists to record his exotic plants and natural history specimens. Ben Franklin said simply of Fothergill: "I can hardly conceive that a better man has ever existed." After his death Fothergill's works were edited by a fellow Quaker and alumnus of St Thomas's, J.C. Lettsom.

John Coakley Lettsom (1744-1815) was not only a friend of John Fothergill but cast very much in the same mould. Hardworking and high-minded, Lettsom also built up a handsome income which he used to nurture his own Garden of Eden at Camberwell. An enthusiastic proponent of Sunday Schools, life-saving, inoculation, fresh air, cheap porridge and free dispensaries, an outspoken enemy of quackery, religious persecution and tea-drinking, Lettsom was satirised by contemporaries as 'Dr. Wriggle'.

Bristolian Quaker J. C. Prichard (1786-1848) was a multilingual polymath who wrote expertly on subjects ranging from epilepsy, Egyptology and etymology to ethnology, which was his principle passion. The overriding conclusion of his far-reaching researches was that on strictly scientific grounds "we are entitled to draw confidently the conclusion that all human races are of one species and one family." Prichard was among the first to advance the then daring idea that white people were in fact descended from black ancestors.

The site of St Thomas's was acquired in 1859 for the extension of London Bridge station and the hospital relocated to its present site, south of Westminster Bridge.

## GUY'S HOSPITAL

Thomas Guy (1644/5-1724) was born in Pritchard's Alley, Fair Street, Horselydown, the son of a carpenter turned coalmonger. Guy established a flourishing bookselling business at

*69. Thomas Guy caricatured as a miser.*

the corner of Cornhill and Lombard Street, became Printer to the University of Oxford and served as MP for Tamworth for twelve years. Single, frugal and shrewd, Guy became rich and used his wealth to generous purposes, relieving many debtors, waifs and refugees and building a town hall and almshouses at Tamworth. In 1704 Guy was elected a Governor of St Thomas's Hospital and three years later endowed three wards there at the cost of £1,000 each. Guy, like most other people with cash to spare, became a subscriber to the South Sea Trading Company which purposed to take over Britain's recently established but rapidly mounting National Debt. By 1720, as speculative frenzy in South Sea stock reached a climax, Guy held £45,500 worth of £100 shares. He began to sell at £300 and disposed of his last holdings at £600, realising some £250,000 as a result. As one of the very few who emerged from the disastrous collapse of the 'South Sea Bubble' in profit, Guy determined to use his fabulous new fortune to establish a new hospital for "four hundred poor PERSONS or upwards, LABOURING UNDER ANY DISTEMPERS, INFIRMITIES OR DISORDERS THOUGHT CAPABLE OF RELIEF BY PHYSICK OR SURGERY; but who, by reason of the small hopes there may be of their

*70. Guy's 'Hospital for Incurables', engraving by John Bowles, 1725.*

cure, or the length of time which for that purpose may be required ... are or may be adjudged or called Incurable and as such not proper Objects to be received into or continued in the present Hospital of Saint *Thomas*".The first phase of Guy's was built between 1722 and 1724. Guy himself was posthumously honoured in 1734 with a bronze statue by the illustrious Scheemakers.

In 1738-9 a new east wing was added to Guy's by the hospital's surveyor, James Steer. This included a committee room and a handsome galleried chapel. In 1744 a 'lunatic house' was added to the accommodation and in 1774-80 a west wing. Cold, hot and vapour baths were installed in 1780. In the same year Thomas Guy was reburied in the hospital's chapel under an exceptionally fine monument by Southwark sculptor John Bacon (*see p105*), for which he was paid an appropriately handsome fee of £1,000. Pevsner has praised it as "one of the noblest and most sensitive of its date in England. It still has the compositional flourish and the technical mastery of the Baroque and Roubiliac, and yet shows the genuine warm feeling of the new age." When prison reformer John Howard toured Guy's in 1788 he praised the new bug-free iron bedsteads and arrangements for ventilation and sanitation. In 1799 Guy's became the first London hospital to appoint a dental surgeon.

72. *Thomas Addison, physician, 1824-60.*

71. *Houses at Guy's Hospital, from 'The Builder', 1863.*

## GUY'S MEN

Of the thousands of distinguished practitioners associated with Guy's space permits the mention of only a handful, notable either for their special eminence or for their close association with the Southwark area.

Richard Bright (1789-1858), appointed to the hospital staff in 1820, is best known for his identification of the kidney condition known as 'Bright's Disease'. Other colleagues who are associated with eponymous conditions were Thomas Addison (1793-1860) and Thomas Hodgkin (1798-1866). Astley Cooper (1768-1841) was appointed Demonstrator of Anatomy at Guy's at the age of twenty-one in succession to his uncle. Elected FRS in 1802, he excelled as a dissectionist, a lecturer and a practical surgeon, attributing his success in the latter field to sheer speed, rather than delicacy of touch. His patients included the Prime Minister, Lord Liverpool, and George IV, who rewarded him with a baronetcy. Charming, handsome and skilled, Cooper was to earn £20,000 a year and serve twice as President of the Royal College of Surgeons. It was Cooper who established a separate medical school at Guy's. The poet John Keats was one of his students.

73.  *Thomas Hodgkin, Curator of the Museum, 1825-37.*

Charles Aston Key (1793-1849) was born in Southwark, the son of a doctor, to whom he was apprenticed. He then trained at Guy's as a pupil of Astley Cooper and went on to become Lecturer

74.  *Sir Astley Cooper, under whom the anatomy school reached its heyday.*

in Surgery at Guy's and personal surgeon to Prince Albert. Key lived at 12 St Thomas's Street from 1821 to 1823. He died of cholera, leaving nine children, one of whom followed him into the profession to become Sir Astley Cooper Key (1821-88).

Walter Cooper Dendy (1794-1871), established his first practice in Stamford Street, where he lived from 1826 to 1839. Surgeon, artist, poet and able public speaker, Dendy published more than a dozen works, including a treatise on dreams and illusions, and had interests ranging from dermatology to anthropology. Despite a reclusive personality, eccentric religious views and a positively bizarre mode of dress, he nevertheless became President of the Medical Society of London.

John Flint South (1797-1882) was the son of the Southwark druggist who took it upon himself to force hartshorn oil between the lips of the dying William Pitt. Having attended the lectures of Sir Astley Cooper, South was appointed conservator of the hospital museum and assistant demonstrator of anatomy, later becoming lecturer. In 1843 he was nominated as one of the first Fellows of the Royal College of Surgeons and twice served as its President. Despite giving the Hunterian Oration without even mentioning Hunter – and giving a survey of the history of surgery which only reached the eighteenth century by the time his time ran out – South did manage to arrange the reinterment of the great anatomist in Westminster Abbey. South spent the last twenty years of his life amassing materials for a monumental history of surgery, which he failed to write.

J.F. South's half-brother was the celebrated astronomer Sir James South (1785-1867), who also trained under the celebrated Cooper. However, marriage endowed him with a fortune which enabled him to give up surgery and establish an observatory in a house in Blackman Street. It was lavishly equipped with a "princely collection of instruments such as have never yet fallen to the lot of a private individual". In 1826 he was awarded the gold medal of the Astronomical Society, of which he later became President. In the same year he moved to Kensington. Despite being knighted and awarded a civil list pension in 1830 South devoted much of his energy in later life to quarrels with fellow astronomers, instrument-makers and builders.

Even as a student Edward Grainger (1791-1824), the son of a Birmingham surgeon, demonstrated a brilliant talent as an anatomist. In 1819 he opened his own anatomy school in attic premises in St Saviour's churchyard, attracting some thirty pupils. It was soon necessary for him to move to larger accommodation, a former Catholic chapel in Webb Street, Maze Pond. The enterprise continued to flourish as Grainger was both an energetic teacher and much favoured by the 'resurrectionists' who kept him supplied with fresh corpses. By 1821 Grainger was able to build his own anatomical theatre and in 1823 an even larger one, for three hundred students. Tuberculosis, aggravated by overwork, claimed him the following year.

William Rendle (1811-93) was initially educated at the British and Foreign Training School in Borough Road (*see p63*) and attended Edward Grainger's medical academy before training at Guy's as a surgeon. He practised for half a century in the Southwark area, serving as Medical Officer of Health for the parish of St George the Martyr between 1856 and 1859. Rendle's private passion was antiquarianism and he distilled his knowledge of the locality into *Old Southwark and Its People* (1878) and *The Inns of Old Southwark and their Associations* (1888).

Sir William Gull (1816-90) not only trained, practised and taught at Guy's but remained associated with it throughout a distinguished career which brought him Fellowship of the Royal Society, honorary degrees from Oxford, Cambridge and Edinburgh, and a baronetcy and appointment as physician to Queen Victoria. Gull was every bit as outstanding as a teacher and public speaker as he was a clinician but his forthright and frequently sarcastic opinions almost certainly cost him the presidency of the College of Physicians. Gull's obituarist notes that he was less popular with the leaders of his profession than with his patients. He died leaving landed estates and a fortune of £344,000.

Samuel Wilks (1824-1911), born in Camberwell, trained at Guy's and subsequently taught there (1856-85) as an authority on pathological anatomy and author of standard texts on diseases of the chest and of the nervous system. Wilks lived at 2 (then 17/18) St Thomas's Street from 1854 to 1860 and at 14 (then 11) from 1861 to 1869. A man of prodigious learning, Wilks drew on his expert knowledge of the history of his discipline to co-author a *Biographical History of Guy's Hospital* and to write an account of the many discoveries made during his long association with his alma mater. Wilks served as President of the College of Physicians (1896-9), was created baronet in 1897

and also appointed physician extraordinary to Queen Victoria.

William Odling (1829-1921) was, like Charles Aston Key, also the son of a Southwark doctor and trained at Guy's. After working as a demonstrator in chemistry he became Lambeth's first Medical Officer of Health and subsequently Professor of Chemistry at the Royal Institution and then at Oxford.

The splendidly named Frederick Henry Horatio Akbar Mahomed (1849-84), born the son of a Turkish bath proprietor in Brighton, proved a prize-winning student at Guy's and seemed destined for a dazzling career, rapidly obtaining appointments at St Mary's, the London Fever Hospital and Guy's itself, gaining qualifications at Brussels and Cambridge and embarking on a major pioneering research project, compiling statistics based on questionnaires sent to GPs around the country. Alas, despite being "possessed of extraordinary powers of work", he was struck down by enteric fever at just thirty-five years of age.

## AMERICAN ALUMNI

James Jackson, of Boston in America, studied under Astley Cooper at Guy's in 1799-1800, lodging "at the house of a hatmaker in St Saviour's Church Yard". On his return to the United States Jackson took with him knowledge of the recently discovered technique of vaccination. He later became Professor of Medicine at Harvard. John C. Warren, another Bostonian, also studied under Cooper at the same time as Jackson. The two men were later to co-operate in founding the Massachusetts General Hospital. Other Cooper disciples included William Gibson, later Professor of Surgery at the University of Pennsylvania, Edward Reynolds, founder of the Massachusetts Charitable Eye and Ear Infirmary and Alexander H. Stevens, who edited an American edition of Cooper's textbook on surgical technique.

## BETHLEM ROYAL HOSPITAL

Bethlem Royal Hospital began as a medieval foundation near Bishopsgate, relocated to Moorfields in 1676 and moved again in 1815 to a site at St George's Fields formerly occupied by the Dog and Duck tavern and spa (see p47). The new asylum consisted of a basement level, surmounted by three storeys and a huge facade of 580 feet. The 122 inmates were brought from the old Moorfields building in hackney carriages. Workshops, laundries and a handsome portico

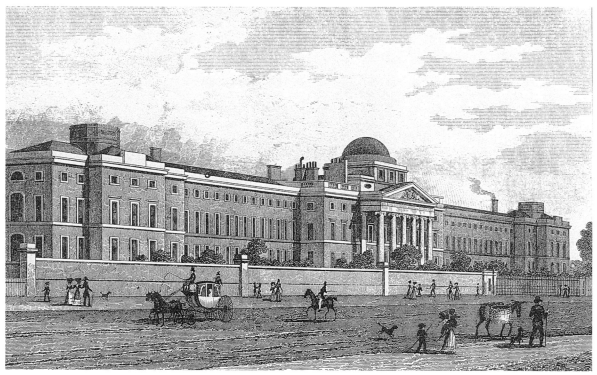

75.  *Bethlem Hospital c.1827, drawn by Thomas H. Shepherd.*

76.  *The Women's Gallery, Royal Bethlem Hospital, 1860.*

*77. Men's Gallery, Royal Bethlem Hospital, 1860.*

and cupola were added to the designs of Sydney Smirke in 1835, the year in which the hospital's accountant fled to the Continent, having embezzled some £10,000. Scandal struck again in 1851 when the death of a patient provoked an official enquiry which was harshly critical of the regime.

The creation of county asylums as an alternative to Bethlem enabled the institution to become more selective in its intake. A new director, Dr. W. Charles Hood, was able to replace brutality with a gentle *embourgeoisement*, introducing a library, social teas and skittles. By 1876 the institution was receiving warm praise from the Lunacy Commissioners.

Celebrated inmates of Bethlem included the painter and patricide Richard Dadd (1819-87) and A.W.N. Pugin (1812-52), architect of the Houses of Parliament and of St George's Cathedral, just opposite the hospital (*see p82*). In 1864 criminal inmates were moved out to Broadmoor. The other patients were moved out to new premises at Addington in 1930. After the residential wings of the hospital were demolished the central block was converted to house the Imperial War Museum from 1936 onwards.

## THE LOCK HOSPITAL

The Lock Hospital, once situated at the junction of Tabard Street and Great Dover Street, was probably founded in the twelfth century to accommodate lepers. It is first mentioned in Patent Rolls of 1315. Its name may derive from the rags (in French *loques*) applied to leprous sores. Administration was taken over by St Bartholomew's Hospital in 1549. John Stow, writing in 1598, refers to "The loke ... a lazar house" but by the eighteenth century the hospital had ceased to treat lepers and was dealing with venereal diseases. It was finally closed in 1760.

## THE EVELINA CHILDREN'S HOSPITAL

This hospital was opened in Southwark Bridge Road in 1869 as a model hospital for children, with thirty beds. The finance came from Baron Ferdinand de Rothschild to honour the memory of his wife, Evelina, who had died in childbirth three years before. The Evelina hospital finally closed in 1975 to be reincarnated on floors 9 to 12 of Guy's Tower.

78. The Lock Hospital for lepers, Kent Street (now Tabard Street).

# Crimes and Punishments

*Five jails or prisons are in Southwark placed*
*The Counter once St Margaret's Church defaced*
*The Marshalsea, the King's Bench and White*
  *Lyon*
*Then there's the Clink where handsome lodgings*
  *be*

John Taylor, 'The Water Poet' 1630

## ROGUES' REFUGE

A royal proclamation of Edward II, dated 1326, declared angrily that "malefactors after their offences flee to Southwark ... out of the city, because the ministers of the city cannot attach [arrest] them there." Two centuries later Richard Foxe, Bishop of Winchester, strongly denied that crime was any worse in his diocese than any other "except for Southwark." In 1595 Nash's *Pierce Penniless* described Southwark as one of five London places of evil reputation. Apart from the rowdiness associated with its function as a red light area, Southwark was also by custom and tradition a bolt-hole for men on the run. In Steen Eiler Rasmussen's blunt phrase "it sheltered the dregs of the City". Former Poet Laureate, translator and plagiarist Nahum Tate (1652-1715) died in Mint Street, hiding from his creditors. Tate's most lasting literary legacy is the Christmas carol 'While shepherds watched ...". He was buried in the churchyard of St George the Martyr. Highwayman and escapologist Jack Sheppard and celebrated 'thief-taker' Jonathan Wild are both said to have sought sanctuary in the Mint shortly before it was suppressed in 1723. In Gay's *The Beggar's Opera* (1728) one of Macheath's gang is known as Mat of the Mint and another character remarks that "the act for destroying the Mint was a severe cut upon our business."

J.M. Beattie's careful study, *Crime and the Courts in England 1660-1800,* chronicles a decline in the murder rate in Southwark of no less than five-sixths between the Restoration and the turn of the eighteenth century. M. Dorothy George in 1925, however, still characterised the area harshly as it was at the latter date – "Kent Street, the Mint and the Clink liberty were particularly bad spots in a squalid district."

79. *Lord George Gordon in St George's Fields, 1780.*

## READY TO RIOT

The existence of a local sub-culture of opportunistic criminality may partly explain the character and course of the Gordon Riots which paralysed the entire capital for days in 1780 until the rioters were shot down by the military. Led by the semi-demented Lord George Gordon (1751-93) a Protestant Association gathered an allegedly immense number of signatures for a petition to Parliament deploring proposals to mitigate the legal and civil disabilities then visited upon Roman Catholics. Supporters of the movement, estimated at up to 60,000 in number, gathered initially in St George's Fields, intending to march on Parliament via Westminster Bridge. But the crowd soon became a mob venting its fury on prisons, breweries and distilleries, institutions which Southwark possessed in unusual abundance. Local results of the rioting therefore included the destruction of both the Clink and the King's Bench. Industrial grievances proved another source of social tension in the area (*see p93-4*).

In February 1855 the *Morning Post* reported an outbreak of what might be called 'social banditry', since it was apparently motivated by a desperation for sustenance, rather than plunder.

> Yesterday, the utmost excitement prevailed among the inhabitants of Tooley Street, owing to the great number of men, dressed in the garb of labourers, parading the streets in gangs of twenty to thirty, levying a species of blackmail on all the shopkeepers of the locality. The bakers' and chandlers' shops seemed to be the places selected for their visits and at 12 o'clock the mob became so outrageous in their demands that most of the shopkeepers were compelled to close their houses.

The superintendent of M Division responded by putting every available policeman onto the streets and arresting the ringleaders of the demonstration.

## KING'S BENCH

The original King's Bench prison stood on the east side of Borough High Street. Conditions were harsh. Prisoners were often kept in fetters because the penalties visited on officers failing to prevent an escape were also harsh. Disease was a hazard for innocent and guilty alike. In 1417 nine prisoners died from pestilence. A pitiful petition of 1624 claimed that eighty prisoners had died of starvation.

In 1554 the martyr John Bradford (?1510-55) was held in King's Bench before execution and in 1670 the theologian Richard Baxter (1615-91) was confined there by Judge Jeffreys for making a paraphrase of the New Testament; but the majority of inmates were felons or debtors. One of the most distinguished was polymath Robert Recorde (?1510-58), whose remarkable career embraced medicine, manuscripts, minting and mining, but chiefly mathematics. It was through Recorde's writings that algebra and the equals

*80. King's Bench Prison, by Pugin and Rowlandson, 1808.*

sign (= , adapted from Latin usage as meaning *est* - it is) were introduced to England. Robert Barker, the King's Printer responsible for the first edition of the 'King James Bible' eventually ran into such business difficulties that he was incarcerated in the King's Bench in 1635 and died there a decade later. In 1653 King's Bench held no less than 399 persons with collective debts of £976,122. Danish sculptor Caius Gibber (1630-1700) was let out every day to work on carving the reliefs on the Monument.

Some inmates were notable for more than their indebtedness. Nathaniel Eaton (?1609-74), President-Designate of Harvard, managed to get himself sacked before the first college building was even completed. A drunkard, embezzler and sadistic thrasher of students, Eaton was judged by the Puritan divine Cotton Mather to be "fitter to be master of a Bridwel than a colledge". This did not prevent Eaton from eventually finding preferment in the English church to become a vigorous persecutor of dissenters and possessor of a rich Devon rectory. Even so, debt claimed him at the last and he died in King's Bench.

The early regime of close confinement gave way, at least for some, to a laxer system which allowed inmates freedom within a circumscribed area known as 'the Rules'. A character in Shadwell's *Epsom Wells* of 1676 remarks that "though marriage be a prison, yet you may make the rules as large as those of the King's Bench, that extend to the East Indies" Defoe, writing in 1722, observed that "its rules are more extensive than those of the Fleet, having all St George's Fields to walk in but the Prison-House is not near so good. By a Habeas Corpus you may remove yourself from one prison to the other and some of those gentlemen that are in for vast sums, and probably for life, choose the one for their summer, the other for their winter habitation...."

Following an enquiry which revealed extortion, drunkenness and other irregularities, and belatedly judged the institution to be "unsafe for the custody and dangerous to the health of the prisoners", the prison was relocated between 1755 and 1758 to new premises at St George's Fields. Distinguished inmates of the new buildings included Tobias Smollett, who wrote *Sir Lancelot Greaves* there in 1758, and John Wilkes (1727-97), whose riotous supporters had to be dispersed with musket fire in 1770.

Burned down in the Gordon Riots of 1780, the prison was rebuilt and became once again notorious for the corruption of its regime, which was

*81. Tobias Smollett, 1721-71.*

lax enough for those who could afford it to bribe the staff. In 1792 a plot to blow it up was foiled. In 1799 a fire, started by accident, gutted the institution.

In 1815 the naval hero Lord Cochrane (1749-1831), unjustly imprisoned for alleged involvement in a Stock Exchange swindle, escaped by means of a rope which broke when he was still twenty feet from the ground. Cochrane nevertheless survived.

Perhaps one of the prison's most colourful inmates was John Mytton (1796-1834), heir to an income of £10,000 a year and £60,000 in cash, who once set fire to his own nightshirt to cure a fit of hiccups. Expelled from both Westminster and Harrow, briefly a hussar, a master of fox hounds and an MP, Mytton, a daredevil rider and crack shot, wrecked the constitution of a Hercules with six bottles of port a day, starting to drink as he shaved himself in the morning. He died in King's Bench of *delirium tremens*, having lost his entire fortune at the age of thirty-seven. Another spectacular wastrel was the splendidly named Sir Lumley St George Skeffington (1771-1850), epitomised by the *Dictionary of National Biography* as a 'fop and playwright'. He was markedly more successful in the former role than the latter. Social success came swiftly in his youth. As a member of the Carlton House set he was treated as an authority on dress by the Prince of Wales and inspired a new colour of cloth 'Skeffington brown'.

82. *A Mock Election in the King's Bench Prison.*

He also numbered among his friends the theatrical greats of his day, including Kemble and Mrs Siddons and was known to visit up to four theatres in a single evening. Skeffington did have some stage success with a melodramatic version of *Sleeping Beauty* but almost all his other efforts failed. Satirised by both Gillray and Byron, he squandered his inheritance so recklessly that he was forced to escape from creditors by living within the Rules of King's Bench until rescued by a modest but timely inheritance. Still wearing false hair and rouged cheeks in old age, he spent his last years as a recluse in lodgings near the School for the Indigent Blind.

Amalgamated to become part of Queen's Bench in the 1840s and used for a time as a military prison, King's Bench was finally closed in 1879 and knocked down in 1880.

## THE MARSHALSEA

The Marshalsea, which originally stood near the present Mermaid Court, is first mentioned in 1373 and was attacked by Wat Tyler's rebels in 1381. The Marshalsea was, in modern terms, a privatised institution, run for profit. Corruption and cruelty were fundamental principles of its regime. In 1504 a mass break-out of prisoners occurred. Those recaptured were summarily executed. Another prison rising, aided by a mob of local apprentices, took place in 1639. Conscience as much as crime or circumstance confined many to the Marshalsea. The dates of neither the birth nor death of John Marbeck are known but it is recorded that he was the organist at St. George's chapel, Windsor in 1541. Such proximity to Henry VIII might have warned a more prudent man against theological pastimes but Marbeck early became a fervent Calvinist and devoted years of secret labour to compiling an English concordance to the Bible. Discovered in 1543 he was confined to the Marshalsea with others, but, unlike his companions, was saved from the stake by the excellence of his musicianship. Marbeck's nine hundred page concordance finally appeared in 1550 after Henry VIII was safely in his grave at St George's chapel, Windsor.

Quick-witted, zealous and arrogant Edmund Bonner (?1500-69) advanced from being a protégé of Cardinal Wolsey to becoming a trusted diplomatic emissary. Appointed to the bishopric of London in recognition of his services in 1539, he fell foul of the Protestant reformers a decade later

*83. The Marshalsea.*

and was confined to the Marshalsea until the accession of Mary Tudor. Restored to his see, Bonner enthusiastically supervised the reinstatement of the Roman liturgy. He was also responsible for the burning of Protestants in both Lon-

*84. Bishop Edmund Bonner*

don and Essex, though not perhaps with the fanatical zeal attributed to him by Puritan martyrologists. A decade after his restoration Fortune's wheel revolved again to return Bonner to the Marshalsea, where he died. He was buried in St George's churchyard at midnight to avoid the possibility of any public demonstration.

The satire *Abuses stript and whipt* (1613), despite its conventional denunciations of Avarice, Gluttony etc., was deemed sufficiently offensive to send its author George Wither (1588-1667) to the Marshalsea, where he composed five pastorals under the title of *The Shepheard's Hunting*. Imprisoned more than once subsequently for his satirical and religious writings, Wither emerged during the Civil Wars to become a significant Parliamentarian, both as a prolific pamphleteer and commander of the strategic stronghold of Farnham Castle. In 1729, when 401 prisoners were incarcerated there, a Parliamentary Committee of enquiry into the Marshalsea uncovered hellish conditions leading to gratuitous deaths from avoidable causes ranging from starvation to suffocation. The inmates included over three hundred debtors whose misery moved philanthropic General Oglethorpe (1696-1785) to raise a special fund to pay off the debts of as many as possible and subsequently to found Georgia as a colony for the resettlement of debtors and petty offenders. John Wesley (1703-91) was appalled by the conditions he encountered in the Marshalsea in

1753 – "Oh shame to man that there should be such a place, such a picture of hell upon earth! ... In the afternoon I visited many of the sick; but such scenes, who could see unmoved!" After removing to premises just north of St George's church, the Marshalsea in 1824 became home to Charles Dickens' father, incarcerated for debt. Dickens himself was hauled out of school in consequence and forced to work in a blacking factory at Hungerford Stairs, dining with his family each evening before going back to lodgings in Lant Street. A stroke of fortune, in the shape of a legacy, released Dickens senior after some months but the interlude left an abiding impression on the future novelist. In 1856 Dickens was to set much of the action of *Little Dorrit* in and around the prison he had come to know personally in such wretched circumstances. The Marshalsea was closed down in 1842.

## THE CLINK
A dockside area replete with pubs and brothels was always bound to be a bit rowdy, which is doubtless why the Bishop of Winchester, indirectly at least proprietor of a number of said establishments, had his own prison, the Clink. First mentioned in 1509, the Clink stood in what

*85. Charles Dickens as a young man, aged 18.*

was then part of the grounds of the Bishop's residence. According to Stow it was used to confine carousers who got out of order in the Bankside brothels. Nearby stood a cage and cucking-stool for the admonition of prostitutes deemed guilty of being a scold or causing an affray. But victims of religious persecution under both Mary and Elizabeth were also held in the Clink. These included the outspoken John Rogers (?1500-55), first Protestant martyr of the Marian persecution, and the controversialist John Hooper, Bishop of Gloucester, both of whom were tried before Gardiner in St Saviour's and executed in 1555. The Jesuit and celebrated exorcist William Weston (1550-1615), was held there from 1586 to 1588 and so was fellow Jesuit John Gerard (1564-1637) who "preferred the Clink to other prisons [he had been transferred from the Counter] on account of the great number of Catholics I found there. Instead of lewd songs and blasphemies, prayers met my ears." Gerard was subsequently transferred again, to the Tower, from which he made a dramatic escape by rope. The Separatists John Greenwood (died 1593) and Henry Barrowe (died 1593), who had been arrested illegally when he came to visit Greenwood, were less fortunate. Although both attained their freedom from the Clink, they subsequently fell foul of their persecutors and perished together at Tyburn.

The Clink's subterranean cells would certainly have been, in the words of the *Survey of London*, "at best uncomfortably damp". It may well have fallen into disuse after 1649 when Winchester House was vacated for subsequent sub-division into tenements. By 1761 it was described as "a very dismal hole where debtors are sometimes confined, but little used". Burned down in the Gordon Riots of 1780, the Clink was not deemed worth rebuilding.

## THE WHITE LION
Surrey's County Gaol took its popular name from what Stow called the "comon hosterie for the receit of travellers "which is known to have existed by 1535 and whose premises it occupied. According to Stow, writing in 1598, "this house was first used as a gaol within these forty years last past."

Like the Marshalsea, the White Lion was run for profit. Under Elizabeth I it housed Catholic recusants and later added the functions of a House of Correction for petty miscreants. The puritan John Udall (1560-92) fell into neither category. A powerful preacher with powerful protectors, Udall criticised the authority - and alleged corruptions - of bishops in the Church of England, openly in his sermons and anonymously in pamphlets. It was the latter which brought him to the White Lion in 1590, ironically under the terms of a statute directed against seditious writings by Catholics. Udall refused to confess or deny his authorship but was found guilty all the same and sentenced to death. Ralegh and Essex, though rivals at court, both tried to intervene on his behalf. An imaginative get-out was then proffered by the Turkey Company which announced its willingness to appoint Udall to a chaplaincy in far-off Syria. Archbishop Whitgift relented and assented. But it was too late. Udall died before he could depart, his health destroyed by the ill usage suffered during his protracted stay in the White Lion. He was buried at St George the Martyr.

Although the White Lion was already judged to be cramped and semi-ruinous by 1666, it was not rebuilt until 1721-4. Its subsequent inmates included felons, Jacobite rebels and Gordon rioters. In 1773 a much improved House of Correction was opened at St George's Fields, with separate facilities for men, women and juveniles, as well as two bath tubs and a designated sickroom. This building remained in use until 1798, after which it became a soap factory. The White Lion was replaced as Surrey's county gaol by Horsemonger Lane, opened in 1799.

## HORSEMONGER LANE GAOL

Surrey's county gaol was built between 1791 and 1799 by local architect George Gwilt the Elder (*see p109*) as a model establishment to accommodate in excess of four hundred prisoners. Its most notorious inmate was, perhaps, murderess Marie Manning (1821-49) whose departure from the world raised an important issue of public policy. Born Marie de Roux in Geneva, she had emigrated to England to work as a domestic servant to two titled ladies and then married a publican. Maintaining a previous relationship with dock worker Patrick O'Connor, Marie invited him to

86. *Horsemonger Lane Jail.*

a meal at her marital home in Bermondsey where she and her husband murdered their guest and buried him under the kitchen floor. Marie then visited O'Connor's Mile End lodgings to steal his railway shares and money. The crime was readily detected by the police and Marie and her husband were duly sentenced to death. As the first husband and wife execution since 1700, the event attracted such an immense crowd that five hundred constables were drafted in to keep order. The sentence was carried out in front of Horsemonger Lane gaol in November 1849. Dickens was among the eyewitnesses and famously wrote to *The Times* to denounce "the atrocious bearing, looks and language of the assembled spectators". To a friend he wrote "I felt I was living in a city of devils". Despite his protest public executions were to continue for almost another twenty years. Maria Manning inspired the villainous Hortense in Dickens' *Bleak House.* Her choice of black satin for her hanging damned that staple of Sunday respectability as a fashion choice thereafter. Horsemonger Lane gaol was closed in 1878 and the buildings demolished in 1880. Newington Recreation Ground, opened by Mrs Gladstone, marks the site.

87.  *St George's Cathedral c.1910.*

# Catholics, Dissenters and Jews

## ST GEORGE'S CATHEDRAL

Provision for Catholic worship in the post-Reformation era became a problem with the growth of a local Irish population in the eighteenth century. As late as 1769 Father John Maloney was arrested for saying Mass in Tabard Street, less than a mile from where St George's Cathedral now stands. In 1786 Father Thomas Walsh managed to hire a room in Bandyleg Walk for £20 a year, but with a softening of anti-Catholic feeling local Catholics acquired in 1793, for £2,000, the use of a chapel – patriotically dedicated to St George – in London Road. Other temporary premises were also used to accommodate refugees from the revolution in France. By 1820 when Father Thomas Doyle (1793-1879) was sent to

London Road from St Edmund's College, Ware, where he had been organist, the local Catholic congregation was reckoned at seven thousand. The passage of the Catholic Emancipation Act in 1829 coincided with the elevation of Father Doyle to become senior priest at what was then known as the Royal Belgian Chapel. By that year the potential congregation was believed to have more than doubled to fifteen thousand. It was largely through Doyle's exertions that in 1839 a committee was established to invite and consider designs for a new church to accommodate 2,500 worshippers, school premises for 500 children and a house for four clergy. The competition was won by the youthful Augustus Pugin (1812-52), who was both a recent convert to the faith and the outstanding exponent of the revived Gothic style. In 1841 to avoid provoking any demonstration of anti- Roman prejudice the foundation stone of the new complex of buildings was laid at a private ceremony staged at seven in the morning. Modelled on the ancient church of

Austin Friars and detailed "in the style of the time of Edward III", the main structure of the new church was completed in 1848. *The Times* was tepid in its enthusiasm, conceding that "if it provokes no censure, it certainly challenges no extraordinary praise." Throughout the course of its construction the architect gave the work his own close personal supervision. Ironically the chosen site was where in 1780 the fanatical followers of the half-demented Lord George Gordon had assembled (*see p75*).

The consecration of St George's was attended by all the English Catholic bishops, plus several others from Scotland, Ireland and abroad, 260 other priests and representatives of the Dominicans, Cistercians, Franciscans, Benedictines, Oratorians, Passionists, and Brothers of Charity. It was an exceptional turnout for an exceptional occasion – the inauguration of the first Roman Catholic cathedral to be built in England since the Reformation. The Protestant Association marked this historic landmark of ecumenism by publishing a pamphlet entitled *The Opening of the new Popish Mass House in St George's Fields*, no doubt assuming that their readers would remember that the Bethlem Lunatic Asylum was nearby.

The first marriage to be solemnized in the church, in 1849, was Pugin's own, his third. Within three years he was to be confined himself in Bethlem, barely a few minutes walk away overlooking his own last great creation.

In 1850, when the papal hierarchy was re-established in England, Cardinal Wiseman (1802-65), a close friend of Father Doyle, was inducted there as the first Archbishop of Westminster and Father Doyle himself was constituted provost of the cathedral chapter of the newly created see of Southwark. The first Catholic Bishop of Southwark was to be Thomas Grant (1816-70) the son of an Irish officer in the British army, who was consecrated in Rome in 1851. Rector of the English College in Rome at the early age of twenty-eight, Grant had played a crucial backroom role in the re-establishment of the English hierarchy, by gathering historical materials and translating masses of documentation into Italian or from Latin. A priest of the greatest simplicity and modesty, he successfully lobbied the authorities to appoint numerous Catholic chaplains throughout the public services.

The schools associated with the cathedral opened in 1854 and the following year the present Notre Dame High School opened on the other side of the road in the charge of two nuns from Namur, thus maintaining the locality's Belgian connection.

In 1871 James Danell DD (1821-81) was installed as Catholic Bishop of Southwark. In 1879 Father Doyle, who had reached a broad Catholic audience through his whimsical correspondence to *The Tablet*, was buried in the cathedral he had done so much to create. The schools were removed in 1887 to make way for a new clergy house. Formal consecration of the church was delayed until 1894. St George's was completely burnt out in 1941. The restoration, completed by Romilly B. Craze in 1953 included unrealised plans for a tower 180 feet high. In 1982 St George's provided the setting for a mass celebrated by the globetrotting Pope John Paul II during the course of his historic visit to the United Kingdom.

## DISSENT

Early modern Southwark, where commercialised sin and conscientious craftsmen co-existed side by side, was exactly the right sort of breeding-ground for nonconformity in all its varieties. Glimpses and fragments only of its tangled local history can be given here. An Independent meeting was certainly in existence locally by 1616, supposedly the earliest congregational church in England. Its first minister, Henry Jacob (1563-1624), had spent over twenty years in exile in Holland. He departed for Virginia in 1622 to be succeeded by John Lothropp (died 1653), who was arrested in 1632 and held for two years in the Clink before fleeing to New England in 1634. In 1637 Henry Jessey (1601-63) took over but the congregation appears to have split up after 1644. Jessey briefly returned to the area as minister of St George the Martyr in 1657-60. Another congregation of Independents was also established in Deadman's Place, surviving until 1788. Members of this congregation followed their minister John Hubbard to Ireland temporarily in 1621, then were briefly in the charge of John Canne (died 1667) who left to head an English congregation in Amsterdam. Thomas Wadsworth (1630-76), who had been born in St Saviour's, was a regular visiting preacher in the 1660s and belatedly returned to his birthplace to die at Pickle Hering Stairs. The noted divine Richard Baxter (*see p76*) then took charge of the congregation for some months. Its burial ground accommodated the mortal remains of Alexander Cruden (1701-70), eccentric author of the celebrated *Concordance* to the Bible.

Benjamin Keach (1640-1704) became pastor of

88. *Exterior of John Bunyan's Meeting House, Zoar Street, Gravel Lane (publ. 1814).*

89. *Interior of John Bunyan's Meeting House when later used by a manufacturer.*

a baptist church in Tooley Street at the age of twenty-eight. In 1672 he established a wooden meeting-house in Goat Yard Passage, Horselydown. This had to be successively enlarged until it could accommodate a thousand worshippers. Keach was an ardent promoter of congregational singing, composed his own hymns and as a spirited controversialist wrote over forty pamphlets and books on sectarian or theological issues. Keach baptised Benjamin Grosvenor (1676-1758) at fourteen. Grosvenor subsequently became assistant to Joshua Oldfield (*see p61*) minister of the meeting at Globe Alley.

During the last year of his life it is claimed that John Bunyan (1628-88), ex-tinker and author of *The Pilgrim's Progress,* preached, at last unmolested, at a Baptist meeting-house then newly built at a cost of £360. It stood in what was then Gravel Lane, now the eastern side of Sumner Street. In the early eighteenth century an alleyway, known as Zoar Street - Zoar meaning refuge or sanctuary - was cut through beside it and the building became known as Zoar Street chapel. Whether or not Bunyan did have a brief associa-

tion with the building, it acquired a further historical significance by housing the earliest nonconformist school in London of which substantial records survive. These reveal that until 1722 Bibles were the only reading-books available but thereafter hornbooks and spellers were purchased for use by the younger pupils. By 1819 the chapel had become a workshop, although the school section survived for some years further. Zoar Street itself was reconstructed in the early nineteenth century and utterly expunged by bombing in World War Two. John Gill senior (1697-1771) was ministering to a baptist congregation at Horselydown in 1719. In 1757 they moved to a chapel near London Bridge. A Dr. John Gill, probably his son, was active in the area in 1791.

Quakers began to meet at the home of Thomas Hackleton near the Falcon Inn from 1658 onwards. James Park (1636-96) a formerly itinerant Quaker preacher who settled in St Olave's, had £12 of his goods distrained in 1683 for absenting himself from parish worship. Between 1674 and 1685 the Quakers gathered at what became known

90. *Interior of Bunyan's School (publ. 1822).*

G. Shepherd del.                                                                    Stow sculp.

VIEW OF THE LATE REV.ᴰ CHARLES SKEL... TON'S MEETING HOUSE ADJACENT TO THE SITE OF THE GLOBE THEA... TRE, MAID LANE, SOUTHWARK.

91.  *Above, interior of the Meeting House used by the Rev. Charles Skelton (1722-98), built adjacent to the site of the Globe theatre.  Below is a mill erected later on its site.*

92. *Unitarian church, Stamford Street. The portico still remains, the rest being demolished after bombing in the Second World War.*

as Old Park Meeting House on land rented from a James Ewer until it was peremptorily seized by the military for use as a guard house. In 1762 they finally found a permanent home in Redcross Street (now Redcross Way), where they remained until 1860.

At Cambridge Etonian Rowland Hill (1744-1833) exhibited the sort of overt religiosity which had won the Wesley brothers the nickname of Methodists at Oxford. Despite being rejected for the priesthood by no less than six bishops, Hill followed his compulsion to become a preacher and from 1783 onwards was based at the Surrey Chapel on Blackfriars Road until his death half a century later. He was eventually to be buried there, at the foot of his own pulpit. Hill's sermons were judged to be "earnest, eloquent, eccentric" and attracted a large and loyal congregation. So did his star organist Benjamin Jacob (1778-1829), whose three hour recitals could attract audiences of up to three thousand and proved excellent fund-raisers for the Rowland Hill Almshouses.

Hill ran thirteen Sunday Schools with an enrolment of three thousand and was a leading member of the Religious Tract Society, British and Foreign Bible Society and London Missionary Society. Vaccination was also one of his

enthusiasms and he carried out thousands of vaccinations himself. The actor Charles Mathews remembered Hill as conspicuously slovenly about his personal appearance: "So inattentive was he to nicety in dress, that I have seen him ... with one red slipper and one shoe, the knees of his

93. *The Reverend Rowland Hill.*

breeches untied, and the strings dangling down his legs."

After Hill's death the 'Rowland Hill Chapel', later 'Primitive Methodist Surrey Chapel, Blackfriars Road', later Octagon Chapel, continued to develop a wide range of ancillary activities, including concerts, lectures, a 'Pleasant Sunday Afternoon Society', men's brotherhood, Band of Hope and Girls' Life Brigade. The congregation finally removed to a new home in Westminster Bridge Road in 1876 and its former home became a factory before being taken over for boxing. Known simply as 'The Ring', it was severely damaged by enemy action in World War Two and demolished in consequence.

Jeremiah Learnoult Garrett was born, the son of Horselydown boat-builders, in 1764. The date of his death is not known. After displaying a precocious childhood avocation for religion, he went through a phase of dissolution which led to a spell in the Lock Hospital. Garrett, chastened and reformed, took to preaching but, after being ejected from Lady Huntingdon's Connection, was obliged to set up a chapel of his own in Lant Street. One of Garrett's sermons was heard by John 'Zion' Ward, inspiring his subsequent ca-

reer as a preacher (*see p65*).

Only the imposing portico of Stamford Street Unitarian Chapel now survives. When the building was first erected a contemporary described it as "chaste and grand". Built in 1821 for a congregation whose lease on a chapel in St Thomas's Street had expired, it came close to closure in 1859 but the congregation was dramatically revived by Robert Spears (1825-99), who served as minister from 1861 to 1874. A self-taught teacher and journalist, Spears was a dynamic organiser with a warm personality and broad cultural interests which made him a pioneer of ecumenism. By 1882 Stamford Street had been so far transformed that the roof of the chapel was taken off so that a hall could be added to accommodate a Sunday School of five hundred children.

Despite his own sketchy education Charles Haddon Spurgeon (1834-92) became a teacher in his early teens and preached his first sermon at sixteen. He made his London pulpit debut at the chapel in New Park Street when not yet twenty and drew such huge numbers that the premises soon had to be enlarged. Spurgeon meanwhile preached to audiences of up to ten thousand

*94. Surrey Chapel, Blackfriars Road.*

95. *Charles Spurgeon.*

crammed into Surrey Gardens music hall. In 1861 a new place of worship was opened specially for him, the imposing Metropolitan Tabernacle at Newington Causeway, built at a cost of £31,000 and capable of accommodating six thousand worshippers. On the completion of his twenty-fifth year there Spurgeon was presented with a testimonial of £6,263. Apart from a four-volume biography he was also memorialized by printed versions of some 2,500 of his sermons.

In the 1890s Charles Booth quoted a baptist minister at length for a description of a typical South London Sunday for the members of his congregation:

> In the morning the man often comes without the wife, leaving her at home to cook the dinner. Sunday dinner, for which all the family are gathered together, takes place between 1 and 2.30. Some children are late for Sunday-school at three because dinner lasts so long. After dinner, when the children go to school, the men sleep, though this has been broken into to some extent by the men's P.S.A. (Pleasant Sunday

Afternoon) meeting lately inaugurated, to which fifty to seventy come, over a hundred being on the books. [The P.S.A. is an Evangelistic service, with instrumental and vocal music, hymns, solos and a short address.] Tea at five and then the evening service, which all attend.

## THE JEWISH COMMUNITY

A synagogue existed in the Borough by the mid-eighteenth century. Geoffrey Alderman, doyen of historians of British Jewry, surmises that it may have come into existence to serve inmates imprisoned for debt. Known as Nathan Henry's Synagogue, it was located behind his house in Market Street and closed following his death in 1853. A second synagogue was founded in 1823 by secessionists (a not uncommon occurrence among London's Jewish community) and located in Prospect Place, St George's Road. Names returned in the census of 1851 suggest a Jewish population of three or four hundred in the Southwark area, mostly employed or self-employed in retailing. From 1867 to 1878 what had by then become known as the Borough New Synagogue was served by the Revd Simeon Singer (1848-1906), a man energetic in charitable causes, notably prison visiting. A preacher of power and eloquence and a protégé of the Rothschilds, Singer was translated from the Borough to Bayswater, i.e. from one of the poorest to one of the wealthiest Jewish communities in the capital. Singer's greatest contribution to British Jewry was his *Authorised Daily Prayer Book,* which rendered a faithful translation of Hebrew into fine English.

Successful Jewish integration into the local community is attested by the fact that Jews habitually voted in parliamentary elections even before they were legally entitled to. In May 1830 Sir Robert Wilson informed the House of Commons that they did so because nobody bothered to enforce the requirement that they should take a Christian oath as the law strictly speaking required. In 1880 the voters of Southwark elected Arthur Cohen QC to represent Southwark (*see p132*). Borough Synagogue continued to flourish and in 1917 M. Rosenbaum published a history of it.

# Making a Living

## A HUNDRED TRADES

The economy of Southwark, like most of London, is now so dominated by service occupations such as medicine, education, finance, catering and retailing, that it is easy to overlook the extent to which both London and Southwark once depended on the actual manufacture of physical products. In Southwark the tradition can be traced back to Roman workers in iron and bronze.

For the later medieval period Martha Carlin's painstaking analysis of the 1381 poll tax returns for Southwark provides a detailed profile of an already highly diversified local economy, involving some 576 identified persons, who between them followed no less than one hundred and one occupations. The single most common occupation was that of tailor (44); other makers of apparel included ten 'schapisters' (seamstresses), six cappers, two makers of points (used for fastening clothes) and a maker of pattens (a sort of light clog used for street wear to protect the shoes). Other associated textile trades involved a comber, a shearman, three dyers, seven fullers, seven 'threadwives', eight weavers and twenty-six spinsters. The leather trades were represented by a tanner, a pouchmaker, two curriers, two girdlers, eight glovers, ten saddlers, fourteen cordwainers (workers in Cordovan i.e. fine leather), fourteen skinners and twenty-one corvisers (cobblers). Clothing in one form or another therefore accounted for some thirty per cent of local employment, females being predominant in this sector. The construction business gave work to twenty carpenters, five masons, three sawyers, two glaziers, a stainer and a tiler; with thirty-nine associated labourers construction thus provided an eighth of local employment. Metal-working involved five smiths, two goldsmiths, two armourers, a bladesmith, a cutler, a grinder and a pewterer. Other specialist craftsmen included a bowyer and a fletcher.

The importance of inns and travellers to the local economy is evidenced by twenty-three 'hostelers' (ostlers), six 'marshals' (farriers), six cooks and two tapsters. The purchasing power of the inns and their customers played a major role in sustaining twenty-five local 'hucksters, at least a dozen self-confessed prostitutes and seven 'stewmongers' plus a substantial range of suppliers of food and drink, including twenty-two brewers and a vintner. Victualling in one form or another accounted therefore for a quarter of all local employment. The fact that there were only six suppliers of bread, four of meat, three each of fish and poultry and none of dairy produce, but that there were four piebakers, three each of specialist dealers in spices and fruit and two in stockfish implies that the bulk of locally consumed basic foodstuffs such as butter, cheese, eggs, milk and bacon were supplied by country people bringing their produce in from the surrounding area.

The other major source of purchasing power was the concentration of substantial, wealthy establishments which could afford to be staffed by thirty-odd female servants, two door porters, a chamberlain and a bailiff. Specialist providers of personal services included six 'lavenders' (washerwomen), four barbers, two 'leeches' and a midwife. The importance of the local ecclesiastical presence is further evidenced in the residence of six clerks and a pardoner. The area's riverside role is reflected in the presence of a ropemaker, four coopers, seven millers and nineteen boatmen. Other transport workers included five 'hackneymen' (keepers of livery horses for hire), five load porters and three carters. The semi-rural character of medieval urban life can also be seen in the presence of a thresher, three haywards, three millwards and ten gardeners.

## A CENTRE OF INNOVATION

The introduction of hop growing in Kent in the fifteenth century gave a renewed stimulus to the already well-established local craft of brewing, as did the influx of Flemish migrants who contributed their own expertise to this business. Flemings were also prominent in the new craft of printing. Coverdale's Bible, the first English version to be printed in England, was produced in 1537 where the Post Office now stands in Borough High Street – "Imprinted in Southwark in St Thomas Hospital by James Nycholson, set forth with the Kynge's most gracious licence." Ex-glazier Nicholson's brother Peter was the King's glazier and responsible, with his predecessors and Southwark neighbours Barnard Flower and Galyon Hone, for making the stupendous stained-glass windows for the chapel of King's College, Cambridge. Treveris Street commemorates the name of local printer Peter Treveris who between 1522 and 1532 published some thirty to forty titles, mostly small grammatical tracts but including one 'Great Herball' and two impor-

96. *Southwark was still pre-eminent in brewing in the nineteenth century and was the logical place to build a magnificent iron and glass Hop and Malt Exchange. This opened in 1867 in the newly constructed Southwark Street – the building still survives. The architect was R.H. Moore.*

tant treatises, one on surgery, the other on chemistry by Hieronymus Braunschweigh. That author's name might tend to imply that Treveris himself was from Trier in Germany. Another theory about this shadowy figure was that he was from the Cornish family of Treffry. Treveris traded at the sign of the 'Wodows' ('Woodwose' = wild man or savage), which also formed part of his logo. The arms of a Sir John Treffry, who fought at Poitiers, incorporated a wild man and woman as heraldic supporters.

By the sixteenth century Southwark was also well established as a location for the manufacture of precision items, such as spectacles and scientific instruments. According to the founder of Garraway's coffee-house, "Nicholas Brook, living at the sign of the Frying-pan in St Tulies-street [i.e. Tooley Street] against the church is the only known man for making of Mills for grinding of Coffee powder ..."

Neither painting nor the making of coffee-grinders was particularly noxious or represented a fire-risk in a densely-packed residential neighbourhood. The same could not be said of other

97. *Fruit baskets piled against eighteenth-century houses at the Borough Market.*

*98. Glassmaking at Apsley Pellatt's Falcon Glassworks. (From 'Curiosities of Glassmaking' by Apsley Pellatt.*

significant local trades such as leatherworking or the manufacture of soap, glass and pottery. Glassmaking, fired by coal brought in along the Thames, began in 1613 in a former brewhouse in the precincts of Winchester Palace. Between *c.*1671 and 1748 another glasshouse was in operation on the site of present-day Benbow House, which takes its name from a later foundry run on the same site by James Benbow and his family. John Bowles opened a glassworks in 1678 at the junction of Deadman's Place (Park Street) and Stoney Street and another near the site of the Rose at Bear

Garden, where in 1691 he began to use what became widely known as 'Crown Glass' (from his trade sign) for window panes. Other typical Southwark glass products included drinking glasses and mirror glass. The Falcon Glass Works was established at the northern end of Hopton Street by the Jackson family in 1688. Their tenure ended in 1752 but the works eventually passed to the firm of Pellatt & Green 'Glass makers to the King'. Under Apsley Pellatt IV (1791-1863) the Falcon works acquired an outstanding reputation. Pellatt, who served as MP for Southwark in 1852-7, became a leading national authority on glassware and took out several patents, including one for 'glass incrustation', i.e. setting decorative medallions and similar items in glass. He also produced experimental lenses for Michael Faraday. An engraving of *c.*1800 also shows an imposing British Plate Glass Warehouse facing onto the Thames just west of Blackfriars bridge.

By the 1620s kilns in Montague Close were producing tin-glazed blue and white imitations of Delft and Ming pottery. Production continued until 1760. From its Bankside origins the production of Delftware spread to nearby Lambeth and distant Bristol and Liverpool. New trades and technologies were not, however, always welcome. In 1675 there were riots against silk-weaving machines. In 1688 washerwomen petitioned the king in protest against pollution caused by the erection of "glasshouses in the middle of the

*99. British Plate Glass warehouse near Blackfriars Bridge.*

100.  *The Anchor Brewery, the most productive brewery in London in the nineteenth century.*

parish to the utter ruin of many of the inhabitants whose livelihood depends upon washing." In Southwark hatters beat an unapprenticed labourer to death. The steam-powered Albion Mills were almost certainly destroyed by arson in 1791 (*see p109*).

## LIQUID HISTORY – THE ANCHOR BREWERY

The first recorded mention of the Anchor brewery at Deadman's Place, Park Street dates from 1633, when its annual ground rent was charged at £21.10.0d and its buildings were valued at £400. The oldest surviving business record, a cash book for 1692, confirms its then owner as James Child, who became Master of the Brewers' Company and whose daughter married Lord Cobham, another Master. By 1710 the brewery was in the possession of Edmund Halsey, who amassed a fortune by supplying beer to the army and is known to have exported beer to Barbados. Halsey served as Master of the Brewers' Company in 1715, as MP for Southwark and as governor of St Thomas's Hospital. His personal papers pro-

vide evidence of a lavish lifestyle. In his will he left £10 not only to each of his household servants but to every single employee as well. Halsey, before his death, had sold the brewery to Ralph Thrale of Streatham, a man of humble origin, who continued to expand the business. On his death in 1758 Ralph was succeeded by his son, Henry, the friend of Dr Samuel Johnson. Thrale, like other leading brewers, lived well, with a villa at Streatham, and indulged in extended jaunts to Bath and the Continent. He likewise undertook the expense as serving as Member of Parliament for Southwark. Apart from Johnson Thrale's house guests in Southwark included Sir Joshua Reynolds, Edmund Burke, David Garrick and Oliver Goldsmith, who had once tried to scrape a living doctoring the poor of Bankside. Thrale succeeded in making the Anchor London's fourth largest brewery but his ambition to join the ranks of the industry's biggest players, producing over 100,000 barrels a year, twice brought the business to the edge of disaster, in 1772 and again in 1778. The scale on which Thrale operated is betrayed by his wife's passing reference in correspondence to her

Barclay could inform a parliamentary committee of enquiry that he represented what could be called, with pardonable pride, the ranks of the "power-loom brewers". Prince Puckler-Muskau, the original of Dickens' Count Smorltork, felt compelled to put the Anchor brewery on his itinerary of unmissable sight-seeing locations. Disaster, in the shape of fire, struck Barclays in 1832 but the brewery was rebuilt and extended to become one of the sights of London. Cunningham's 1850 *Handbook of London* dilated upon its stupendousness – "The establishment in Park-street is now the largest of its kind in the world. The buildings extend over ten acres and the machinery includes two steam-engines. The store-cellars contain 126 vats, varying in their contents from 4,000 barrels down to 500. About 160 horses are employed in conveying beer to different parts of London."

## WORKSHOP AND FACTORY

The Anchor was a large, capital-intensive business, sprawling over an extensive site. Other substantial Victorian enterprises in Southwark included Clowes' printing works, Potts and Sarson's vinegar works, Crosse and Blackwell's pickle factory, Epps Steam Cocoa Mills and Day and Martin's factory for making shoe polish. In

*101. Dr Johnson taking tea with Mrs Thrale in the Borough, c1770-80.*

own mother's "little savings" of £3,000. Henry Thrale died in 1781. Johnson, acting as one of Thrale's executors, helped to arrange the sale of the brewery to the Barclays banking family, who entrusted it to Thrale's very capable manager, Perkins. Johnson seems to have enjoyed his role in this transaction, asserting with uncharacteristically zestful hyperbole that "we are not here to sell a parcel of boilers and vats but the potentiality of growing rich beyond the dreams of avarice".

The Barclays were one element in what Thrale's widow deftly summarised as "a knot of rich Quakers", which embraced the Bevans and the Gurneys, all of whom were linked together by cousinage and intermarriage. Johnson's visionary hype turned out to be an accurate prediction. By 1810 the Anchor brewery was turning out 235,000 barrels annually and by 1830 Charles

*102. The Anchor Pub, 1948.*

Ewer Street could be found Easton and Amos, who made the waterworks for Trafalgar Square's fountains, while Cole's made cranes in Sumner Street. As early as 1843 G. Dodd's *Days in the Factories* could characterise the area thus:

> An array of tall chimneys, each one a guide post to some large manufacturing establishment beneath – here a brewery, there a sawmill, farther on a hat factory, a distillery, a vinegar factory and numerous others. Southwark is as distinguishable for its tall chimneys and clouds of smoke emitted by them, as London is for its church spires.

Much Southwark industry, however, remained on a workshop scale. Hat-making, a craft associated with the area for centuries, had been revolutionised in the 1830s when beaver was replaced by silk as the fashionable material for headgear at the top end of the market. Over time the range of output was further extended to ladies' bonnets, cloth caps, pith helmets and the celebrated 'Bowler hat'. This was invented by Thomas Bowler of Southwark Bridge Road, originally as a more practical substitute for the top hat, to be worn while hunting. Of the 3,506 hatters working in Southwark in 1841, 2,600 were men over 20,600 were women and 300 children. Many of them had been recruited from traditional textile-making

areas in Gloucestershire and Lancashire. A few were French. Writing in 1850 investigative journalist Henry Mayhew noted the concentration of the trade in the locality.

> The hat manufactories of London are to be found in the district to the left of the Blackfriars Road (as the bridge is crossed from the Middlesex side), stretching towards and beyond the Southwark Bridge Road towards the High Street, Borough and to Tooley-street.

The 1872 Ordnance Survey map of Southwark reveals numerous warehouses and stores for ale, leather and rags as well as the stoneyards, timber yards and sawmills one might expect of a riverside location. The processing of imported materials such as sealskins, furs, coconut fibre, hair and flock was widespread. The rendering of tallow and manufacture of boots and shoes were clearly linked with the leather trade in neighbouring Bermondsey, just as brewery waste was recycled locally to make oilcake and vinegar. Much of the output of the area's many iron foundries may also have been consumed locally in the manufacture of 'architectural ironmongery', carts and wheels, iron bedsteads, coal hole covers, guns, cranes, railway signals and boilers. Other local products included whitelead and blacklead, candles, starch, soap, oilcloth and carpets.

*103. Chamberlain's Wharf and Warehouses, 1830. Watercolour by T.H. Shepherd.*

Commerce was important as well as manufacturing. Along Tooley Street there were twelve dealers in potatoes, eight in cheese, one in 'Irish provisions' and others in ham and tea, paper, pipeclay, lead, coal, slate, sheet glass and alum. There were also manufacturers of tarpaulin, gaugers' instruments, ship's biscuit, chronometers and dog food. At the London Bridge end of the street were two hotels, the Bridge House and the Terminus. Given the insalubrious character of their surroundings their clientele is likely to have been overwhelmingly of a commercial character. The Terminus, with 150 rooms, lasted from 1861 to 1893 as an hotel and was then converted to offices which were destroyed by bombing in 1941.

Many Southwark residents, such as clerks, shop assistants, office cleaners and dock-workers journeyed elsewhere in the capital to their employment. A contemporary noted that "The bulk of the workers travel ... often across the river to their daily task. Morning and evening see the bridges crowded with those who pass their working day in London so much that it is difficult to cross at all against the stream which sets northwards in the morning and southwards at night."

The complexity and sophistication of the metropolitan economy by 1914 can be illustrated by the remarkable range of specialised businesses to be found in Southwark Street alone. They included a hotel valuation specialist, a public house broker, a firm of artesian well engineers, a milking machine engineer, type founders and manufacturers of webbing, cotton belting, mineral water machinery, brushes and Christmas cards. Proximity to Guy's Hospital may explain the presence of makers of enamelled holloware, hygienic appliances and breathing apparatus. Other enterprises included the Leather Trades Publishing Company, the Imperial Food Preservation Company, the National Envelope Company and the American Cockroach and Blackbeetle Solvent Company, which was doubtless attracted by the potential market represented by the large number of warehouses and food-processing establishments in the surrounding area.

Much industry was destroyed by German bombing in World War Two. But Southwark retained its predominantly industrial and commercial character. Indeed volume XXII of the *Survey of London*, covering Bankside, refers to it as "a gloomy and crowded area of wharves and factories". The artwork on the cover of the *South-*

*104. Henry Wilson's tea warehouse at the London Bridge end of Borough High Street.*

*wark Official Guide* published in the late 1940s, depicts the area around the Cathedral on an optimistically sunny day and features brawny Cockneys in flat caps, one driving a horse-drawn flat-bed wagon piled with sacks, another carrying a wicker basket of fruit on his head. The advertisements inside suggested a local economy still more attuned to the industrial age. Grey and Marten proclaimed their lead and solder works to be 'A Southwark Landmark!'. Other major employers included Letts, a name synonymous with diaries and calendars since 1816, Sainsbury's at 13-15 Stamford Street, Mecca Catering, and Dolcis Shoes in Great Dover Street. The engineering firm of Dewrance & Co, established in 1844, proudly proclaimed its founder as the eponymous John Dewrance, erector of George Stephenson's celebrated locomotive 'The Rocket'. Characteristic manufactures of the area included printing machinery, office furniture, pumps and valves, envelopes and packaging, confectionery, perfumes, paints and glue, twine, sacks and belting, rubber boots and industrial clothing. The persistence of wartime shortages was betrayed in the assurance by one advertiser that "supplies of Wallpaper, Paint and Distemper are still very limited but our customers are assured that the

*105. An active scene in the cellars of Max Greger Ltd of Great Guildford Street. The main product sold was a drink called Carlowitz. (From the Pictorial World, 3 March 1883.)*

*106. Boning meat at J Sainsbury's new factory, 1936. (Sainsbury Archives)*

available stocks will be distributed as fairly as possible." Civic pride shone through in the confident assertion that "all the world is familiar with such Southwark products as Galloway's Cough Mixture, Collis Browne's Chlorodyne and Wright's Coal Tar Soap". Sherley Dog Powders were described as 'far-famed' from their home in Marshalsea Road. There was even a passing tribute to the "fine craftsmanship which produces a Hangman's Rope."

Manufacturing in north Southwark was, however, soon in full retreat. Between 1966 and 1974 local manufacturing jobs declined by a precipitous 38%. Sainsbury's closed down much of their Stamford Street operation in 1973. Hayward Brothers, who had been manufacturing coal-hole covers in Union Street since 1848, closed their doors in 1976. The Park Street brewery ceased production in 1982.

# Parish Churches, Ancient and Modern

## ST OLAVE

St Olave in Tooley Street, at the foot of London Bridge on its eastern side, certainly existed by 1096. It was originally controlled by the Warenne earls of Surrey and passed from them to the Prior of Lewes. It had a churchyard on its northern side and both were subject to constant flooding. Despite its awkward location St Olave's developed as a focus of intense Catholic devotion with a strong musical tradition, having a choir and two organs. Five guilds dedicated to the devotion of particular saints were based in the church, a remarkable number considering that there were only just over eighty such guilds in all London. In 1541 St Olave's had a curate and four more stipendiary priests but between 1546 and 1552 this stronghold of Catholic fervour underwent a religious revolution. The guilds were dispossessed of the properties which supported their activities, books in Latin, a fine monstrance and much plate were sold off and images of saints, the rood screen and the churchyard cross were taken down. Altars were replaced by a communion table. Brass plates were taken off the graves and grudgingly passed back to whichever family might care to claim them. An English Bible was purchased and the

*107. The Norman church of St. Olave. An early eighteenth-century engraving.*

Ten Commandments painted up. During Mary's brief reign Catholic traditions of worship were enthusiastically reinstated together with the rood and cross and even the brasses on the graves. A final stripping of the altars followed under Elizabeth and by the 1580s the churchyard was being used for drying clothes – four pieces for a penny. St Olave's was rebuilt in the 1730s to the designs of Henry Flitcroft (1679-1769), architect of St Giles-in-the-Fields. By the early nineteenth century the rectory adjacent to the church was deemed uninhabitable and leased off to a girls' charity school. From 1827 to 1846 St Olave's was fortunate to have as its organist the outstanding talent of Henry John Gauntlett (1805-76). The church was finally demolished c.1928.

## ST MARGARET

This small church was certainly in existence by 1129 and may date back to 1107. Controlled by St Mary's, it was home to two guilds, one of which was devoted to London's own saint, Thomas Becket, the other being the Fraternity of the Assumption of the Virgin Mary. The day of its patron saint, 20 July, was marked with junketings which included a bonfire, hired professional singers, a procession, the distribution of bread, ale and wine and, in the mid-fifteenth century, the performance of a play as well. An inventory of 1485 testifies to the wealth of the parish in listing silver and gilt crosses, chalices, censers, candlesticks, bells and reliquaries, embroidered banners, altar cloths and frontals, hearse and grave cloths, splendid vestments, including one set valued at £110 and books to the value of £102. St Margaret's was vacated at the Reformation and its site sub-divided for various uses, including the Counter (local debtor's prison) a tavern and shops. A former chapel was leased out to support St Saviour's grammar school and the southernmost part used as a court-house before being torn down for a town hall to be built on its site in the reign of James II. The town hall was itself demolished in 1793 to make way for a bank which, at the time of writing, has been reincarnated as a fashionable brasserie.

## ST GEORGE THE MARTYR

This church is first documented in 1122 and was rebuilt at the end of the fourteenth century. Henry V stopped to pray there en route to France and the bloody siege of Harfleur where, according to

108.  *St Olave's Church in 1810, as rebuilt by Henry Flitcroft.*

109. *St George the Martyr Church, c1925.*

Shakespeare he would link his name with that of England's patron saint as a single battle-cry.

St George's has traditionally been associated with the Skinners', Grocers', Drapers' and Fishmongers' Companies. It had three chantry priests and from 1510 until his death in 1527 the rector was the Italian poet Peter Carmelianus, former chaplain and Latin secretary to Henry VII and Lute Player to Henry VIII. Carmelianus, a protégé of Caxton and friend of Erasmus, was a pluralist, holding church appointments in Yorkshire and Westminster and land in Surrey, so it is likely that he took little personal interest in St George's. From 1615 until his death the rector was the astronomer and mathematician Edmund Gunter (1581-1626), inventor of a small portable quadrant. In 1619 he was appointed professor of astronomy at Gresham College. Gunter made important contributions to the art of navigation by devising mathematical tables and conducting experiments on the variation of the magnetic compass. He also introduced Gunter's chain, used in land surveying.

The church was enlarged, "new pewed and beautified" in 1629, perhaps as part of Laud's campaign to revivify the formalism of English worship. In 1653 General Monk (1608-70), future architect of the Restoration, married his laundress, Anne 'Nan' Radford at St George's.

Although a restoration had been undertaken in 1715-16, St George's was completely rebuilt by John Price between 1734 and 1736, the work being funded by a parliamentary grant under the terms of the Fifty New Churches Act passed a quarter of a century previously. Pevsner commended the outcome as "a sound, sturdy church, uncommonly well sited" so that its tower appears to advantage from north and south alike.

110. *St George's, drawn by Arthur Moreland in 1931.*

From 1749 until his death the rector was Leonard Howard (?1699-1767) who rose from the obscurity of clerking in the Post Office to become chaplain to the Prince of Wales and subsequently to the Princess Dowager of Wales. Despite simultaneously holding lectureships at two City churches, Howard's improvidence obliged him to spend several terms in King's Bench, where his somewhat abused talents as a writer led fellow inmates to dub him their 'poet laureate'. Although he did actually publish a number of devotional works, Howard tended to use his literary career as a device for raising subscriptions for works that were destined never to appear. He was, however, able to trade on his pleasing personality to remain popular with his parishioners. He was buried at St George's.

In 1776 a resolution was passed at a public vestry meeting "to sell to Mr Samuel Carter all the parish papers and documents in a lump, at the rate of three half-pence per pound, he being at the expense of carrying them away."

St George's churchyard was converted to a public garden in 1882. In 1897 Basil Champneys installed a spectacular ceiling. The restoration of 1951-2 included the installation of a stained-glass east window incorporating the figure of Dickens' *Little Dorrit* whom the author has both baptised and married in St George's.

## ST MARY MAGDALENE

St Mary Magdalene was created some time between 1220 and 1238 to serve the lay residents of the St Mary's priory precinct. Its dedication may well strike one as a reference – or reproach – or even invitation to the nearby inhabitants of the stews (*see p43*). The poet John Gower (*see p111*) bequeathed to the church ten shillings for the priest and forty shillings to be spent on candles and ornaments. St Mary Magdalene was merged with St Margaret's in 1540 to create the new parish of St Saviour.

## ST THOMAS IN THE HOSPITAL

St Thomas was originally the hospital chapel but acquired parochial functions between 1492 and 1496. The parents of diarist John Evelyn were married there in 1613. The church was rebuilt in 1702. Its garret was used by the hospital to store dried medicinal herbs, then as an overflow ward and finally in the early nineteenth century to house a lecture theatre for demonstrating surgical techniques (*see illustration 67*). This operating theatre was subsequently walled up and so completely forgotten that its rediscovery in the course of maintenance work in 1956 caused a minor sensation. It has since become one of the area's most popular visitor attractions.

## CHRIST CHURCH

John Marshall of Axe Yard died childless in 1631, leaving £700 for the erection of a new church within the parish of St Saviour's. Forty years were to pass before his bequest was acted upon and a separate parish of Christ Church established in 1671, corresponding to the manor of Paris Garden. A church was built and consecrated that same year, although the spire was not completed until 1695. The consecration was performed by John Dolben (1625-86), Bishop of Rochester, an ecclesiastical celebrity of the first rank. An ardent

*111. Christ Church, an engraving published in 1770.*

Royalist, Dolben had broken off his undergraduate studies at Oxford to fight at Marston Moor and in defence of York, being twice wounded and promoted major. As Dean of Westminster he had during the Great Fire of 1666 rounded up a hundred boys from Westminster School and formed them into a bucket-chain to save the church of St Dunstan-in-the-West. A fine extempore preacher of commanding presence, the genial and popular Dolben subsequently became Archbishop of York. He is commemorated in Dolben Street, off Bear Lane.

Although the church had a number of attractive features such as Tuscan columns, a wainscoted nave and a gallery, it had been erected in haste on marshy land, with insufficient attention to its foundations and drainage. By 1721 it was reported to be "in a very decaying condition, both withinside and without"; as it had sunk so far that its windows were virtually at ground level this was scarcely an exaggeration. The churchyard had also proved too small to cope with a considerable 'increase of the Inhabitants' and those graves that could still be dug were becoming waterlogged before they were even finished. In 1735 a garden was purchased as a new burial ground and between 1738 and 1741 the entire church was rebuilt "very plain, but neat". The churchyard had to be enlarged again in 1817-19. A watch-house to guard against grave-robbers was erected in the latter year. Extensive restoration to and enlargement of the church building took place in 1870-1 and 1890-1. In 1895 it was discovered that heat from the boilers had melted so many lead coffins in the vault that 652 bodies had to be removed and reinterred at the necropolis in Woking.

Christ Church was completely gutted by bombs in 1941. The chancel was patched up sufficiently to hold services and incorporated into a second rebuilding in 1959-60. As befits a church which endured the ordeals of 'the People's War', the reconstructed building contains a pleasingly democratic portrayal in its stained-glass windows of typical workers of the Southwark area, from the printer to the cleaning lady.

## ST JOHN'S, HORSELYDOWN

This parish was created in 1733. For many years the organist was James Hook (1746-1827) who also played nightly at Vauxhall. Hook composed some two thousand songs, most notably *The Lass of Richmond Hill*.

## VICTORIAN EXPANSION

The rapid expansion of population in Southwark throughout the nineteenth century prompted the building of new churches. An 1854 report on the 1851 census of religious worship showed that St Saviour could accommodate only 25% of the population which it was supposed to serve.

St Peter's church in Sumner Street was consecrated in 1839. It had been built on land donated for the purpose by Potts, the vinegar manufacturers and was described as "a handsome, though not very richly adorned, specimen of Gothic architecture". The architect was a local man, Christopher Edmonds. Given the date, St Peter's would have been a fairly early example of the 'Gothic Revival' then gathering pace under the influence of Pugin's *Contrasts*. St Peter's could hold a congregation of up to 1,200. It was totally destroyed by bombing in 1940. All Hallows, Pepper Street, built to designs by George Gilbert Scott jnr in 1880, was also to be totally gutted in the Blitz.

Other Victorian foundations included St Stephen, Manciple Street (S.S. Teulon, 1850), St. Michael's, Lant Street (A.S. Newman, 1867) and St. Alphege's, Lancaster Street (R. Willey, 1876) where the Rev. A.B. Goulden (d.1894) became known as 'the costers' bishop'. The concentration of poverty in the area also attracted the attention of external agencies recruited from the ranks of the social elite. The Charterhouse Mission, supported by the famous City school which had relocated in leafy Godalming, was established in Tabard Street in 1884; its mission church, St Hugh's was consecrated in 1898. The Women's University Settlement opened its doors in Nelson Square in 1891.

# The Arts

## SCULPTURE

Although their dates of birth and death have been lost, the Janssen family, of Flemish extraction, are known to have been Southwark residents, in the parish of St Thomas the Apostle. Bernard Janssen (*floruit c.*1610-30) was employed as master mason of Northumberland House in the Strand and Audley End in Essex and worked with Nicholas Stone, the most successful native funerary sculptor of his day, on the tomb of Thomas Sutton in the Charterhouse. Geraert Jansen, who Anglicized his name as Gerrard Johnson, and may have been Bernard's brother, is noteworthy for producing in 1616 the posthumous portrait bust of Shakespeare which can still be seen in Holy Trinity, the parish church of his native Stratford-on-Avon. The imposing monument to Lancelot Andrewes (*see illustration 37*) in Southwark Cathedral is also attributed to the Janssen atelier.

William Cure (died 1632) was the son of Cornelius Cure (died 1607), a Dutchman, and was born in the parish of St Thomas the Apostle, Southwark. Cornelius, successively master-mason to Elizabeth I and James 1, was commissioned to erect the monuments to Elizabeth I and Mary, Queen of Scots in Westminster Abbey. Following the death of his father William Cure completed the monument to Mary Queen of Scots, receiving the huge sum of £825. 10s for his share in the work. William Cure went on to complete funerary monuments for Sir Roger Aston, Master of the Great Wardrobe, James Montague, Bishop of Winchester and in Southwark Cathedral local worthy Alderman Richard Humble (died 1616). He also worked on the Banqueting House in Whitehall for Inigo Jones until his death, when he was succeeded as master-mason by Nicolas Stone. Cure was buried in the church of St Thomas the Apostle.

From about 1680 until the end of his life Thomas Cartwright the Elder (*c.*1617-1702) was employed on the adornment of St Thomas's Hospital, supplying figures of 'fower cripples' and of King Edward VI. He also served as master mason on the rebuilding of the parish church of St Thomas at Southwark. Cartwright was twice Master of the Masons' Company and worked on many Wren churches and Livery Company Halls after the Great Fire.

According to the *Daily Journal* of 10 March 1731, Batty Langley (1696-1751) had "a stone warehouse at Bankside at the sign of the Hercules Head in Southwark". Langley supplied statues, sundials, seats, carved shields, columns and stucco ornaments. He also invented a kind of artificial stone for making friezes and cornices and was described by the art historian George Vertue as "a bold-faced undertaker". Langley is, however, often better remembered as a prolific writer on practical aspects of building and garden design.

The statue of James II which adorned Southwark Town Hall (*see illustration 112*) between 1685 and 1793 was carved by the eccentric John Bushnell (died 1701), whose twenty-two years experience working in Italy had made him notoriously arrogant but also won him commissions to carve statues for the Royal Exchange.

Thomas Dunn (*c.*1676-1746) was a pupil of David Farmer of Southwark and served as mason-contractor to Nicholas Hawksmoor on building Christ Church, Spitalfields and St Mary Woolnoth in the City. He also worked on Greenwich Palace and the Mansion House. Dunn's yard in Blackman Street also turned out chimney-pieces for distinguished clients such as the Royal Physician, Dr Richard Mead (*see p66*) and the banker Benjamin Hoare.

John Bacon (1740-99) was born in Southwark, the son of a clothworker and initially apprenticed as a modeller in a china factory, later graduating to Mrs Coade's artificial stone establishment at Lambeth. Entering the Royal Academy in 1768 as one of its earliest intake of students, he became the first to win its Gold Medal for sculpture and in the same year modelled for Wedgwood. He was elected RA in 1777. George III himself recommended Bacon to create the massive monument to the Earl of Chatham in Westminster Abbey. Bacon's other major monuments include the statues of Dr Johnson, John Howard and Sir William Jones in St Paul's Cathedral and the spectacular funerary tribute to Thomas Guy in Guy's Hospital chapel (*see p69*). Self-taught, Bacon left £60,000 at his death. Bacon's equestrian statue of William III in St. James's Square was finished by his sons. The younger son, John, made a fortune out of mass-producing rather uninspired monuments and tablets, trading on his father's famous name.

Of Emanuel Williams little more is known except that he worked as a mason and carver in Tooley Street and went bankrupt in 1778, having just completed the west wing and centre building of Guy's.

*112. Southwark Town Hall, St Margaret's Hill, showing the statue of James II carved by John Bushnell.*

## PAINTING

Irishman Robert Barker (1739-1806) is credited with inventing the panorama, though he may only have introduced to England a pre-existing Continental invention. Sir Joshua Reynolds pronounced such a project so impracticable that he vowed to get up in the night to view it if Barker succeeded. In the event when news of its completion was brought to him he was sporting enough to admit his error, abandon his breakfast table and walk in his dressing-gown and slippers to Leicester Square to inspect it and pronounce it a success. Barker went on to produce panoramas of the fleet of Spithead and a celebrated view of London, painted from the roof of the Albion Mills in Southwark. Having patented his invention successfully, Barker acquired permanent premises in Leicester Square and proved so successful that he was able to buy out his backers. Barker eventually died at his home in West Square.

"Had Tom Girtin lived, I should have starved," the great Turner once generously observed of his boyhood friend. Thomas Girtin (1775-1802) was born the son of a Southwark rope-maker. The achievement of his all too brief career was nothing less than to revolutionize the art of watercolour painting. Before Girtin this amounted essentially to tinting sketches which had already been drawn in detail in pencil. Girtin made watercolour itself the main medium. Turner was one of the few talented enough to follow him almost at once. Ruskin thought Girtin a decisive influence on Turner's early development. Girtin's worldly success was severely limited by his indifference to polite society and his adamant refusal to augment his income by tutoring talentless amateurs.

Benjamin Haydon (1786-1846) aspired to artistic greatness and was certainly gifted at self promotion but was fatally handicapped by an appalling incapacity to handle his finances and a lifelong tendency to bite the hands that occasionally attempted to feed him. June 1827 saw him imprisoned for debt in King's Bench for the second time. Artistic opportunism triumphed over despair as he surveyed his fellow inmates, the human

*113. Benjamin Haydon, 1786-1846.*

detritus of the world capital of capitalism.

> What a set of beings are assembled in that extraordinary place! - that Temple of Idleness and debauchery! ...Good God! When you walk amongst them, you get amongst faces that are all marked by some decided expression, quite different from people you meet in the street.

Haydon witnessed an extraordinary and bizarre theatrical occasion as his fellow inmates, who had organised themselves into a sort of theatrical company to while away the time, enacted a mock election (*see illustration 82*), beginning with a procession, to choose two MPs to plead for their rights before the House of Commons. Haydon was seized with emotion at the sight of dozens of London's economic casualties "forgetting their sorrows at the humour, the wit, the absurdity of what was before them the finest subject for honour and pathos on earth." His subsequent painting, *The Mock Election,* was exhibited at the Egyptian Hall on Piccadilly in 1828 and bought by King George IV for five hundred guineas. In 1832 Haydon was commissioned by Lord Grey for a like sum to paint *The Reform Banquet* held in Guildhall to mark the passage of the Act of that year reforming the parliamentary franchise. It proved a transient triumph. Haydon continued to be dogged by debt and professional frustration and committed suicide at sixty, leaving a wife and six children. The posthumous publication of his witty and perceptive diaries revealed that he had mistaken his métier all along.

Solomon Joseph Solomon (1860-1927) was born in the Borough, the fourth son of a leather merchant. Elected to the Royal Academy in 1906, Solomon was noted for classical and biblical subjects and portraiture. His sitters included Jewish novelist and educationist Israel Zangwill, actress Mrs Patrick Campbell and Labour premier Ramsay MacDonald. Solomon used his expertise to life-saving effect as the government's special adviser on camouflage during the Great War. He also served as President of the Royal Society of British Artists.

The Borough Polytechnic became the last refuge of David Bomberg (1890-1957) as he turned from the commercial failure of his career to embrace teaching with a passion. The son of Polish immigrants, Bomberg was trained by Sickert and at the Slade, knew Wyndham Lewis and travelled to Paris with Epstein to meet Picasso. After serving in the Royal Engineers during the Great War, Bomberg travelled widely to paint in Palestine, Petra, the Soviet Union and Cyprus but most of all in Spain. Teaching at Borough Polytechnic between 1945 and 1953, he was a member of the 'Borough Group' (1947-9) and the 'Borough Bottega' (1953-5) and numbered among his pupils Frank Auerbach and Leon Kossoff. Bomberg passed his final years in obscure poverty and died in St Thomas's.

*114. David Bomberg, c.1912.*

# Architects and Engineers

## FATHERS AND SONS

Robert Mylne (1734-1811) was one of that able army of ambitious Scots who made their way to London in the century after the Act of Union. Born into an Edinburgh family who had been masons for five generations, Mylne was apprenticed to his father the city's Surveyor. At twenty he travelled to Rome, where he studied for four years and became the first British winner of the gold and silver medals for architecture of St Luke's Academy. Returning to London, he submitted a design for the competition to design a new bridge at Blackfriars and, despite being a stranger in the capital and only in his mid-twenties, won. Contemporary cartoonists alleged backstairs influence by Lord Bute, a fellow Scot. Work began in

116. *Robert Mylne, F.R.S., (1734-1811).*

115. *Blackfriars Bridge under construction, from an engraving by Edward Rooker, 1766.*

1760 and was completed in 1769, under budget. Mylne also achieved the laying out of St George's Fields with similar economy and efficiency (*see p35*). In 1780 he designed and built himself a house on the east side of Great Surrey Street, as Blackfriars Road was known until 1829. After his death the house became the York Hotel before it was demolished in 1863. Mylne's other London projects included wings for Northumberland House, the City of London's Lying-In Hospital, Almack's Rooms in St James's and offices for the New River Company in Clerkenwell. His country projects included houses in Hertfordshire, Oxfordshire and Nottinghamshire and bridges at Hexham, Glasgow and Newcastle. Mylne also designed a drainage project for the fens which was carried out after his death by his compatriot and near neighbour John Rennie. A Fellow of the Royal Society, a friend of Dr Johnson and Surveyor of St Paul's, Mylne was buried in the cathedral near Sir Christopher Wren, whose memory he venerated. *The Dictionary of National Biography* notes of Mylne that he was "the last architect of note who combined to any great degree the two avocations of architect and engineer."

George Gwilt (1746-1807), a protégé of the brewer Thrale (*see p94*), became district surveyor for St George's parish and built the Surrey County Bridewell at St George's Fields in 1772 and Horsemonger Lane gaol between 1791 and 1798. He also built houses in Union Street, himself living in one of them, no.18 (then 8). Gwilt's eldest son, George Gwilt the Younger (1775-1856), was born in Southwark, trained by his father and lived in his Union Street house. Like John Newman (see below) Gwilt reserved his real passion for archaeology rather than architecture and he turned part of his home into a museum of local antiquities. Gwilt's greatest professional achievement – a pure labour of love – was the restoration of the tower and choir of St Mary Overie between 1822 and 1825 at a cost of £35,000. Gwilt's younger brother, Joseph (1784-1863) had the professional advantage of a formal training in the Royal Academy Schools. Joseph Gwilt was responsible for building the approaches to Southwark Bridge and succeeded his father as Surrey's County Surveyor. He is chiefly remembered, however, as a prolific author on architectural topics. His publications included a pioneering work on shadows in architecture and a comprehensive encyclopaedia of architecture which first appeared in 1842 and ran through three more editions between 1851 and 1859.

117. *John Rennie, 1761-1821, drawing by George Dance.*

John Rennie (1761-1821), a Scottish farmer's son, was educated at the University of Edinburgh and initially worked as a millwright under his compatriot Andrew Meikle, inventor of the threshing-machine. In 1784 the young Rennie so impressed James Watt that he was commissioned to design the machinery for the pioneering Albion Flour Mills on the Southwark side of Blackfriars Bridge, for which the firm of Boulton & Watt was supplying the steam-engines. By the time the stupendous Mills had become one of the sights of London Rennie had broadened his interests from mechanical to civil engineering and in 1791 settled in Stamford Street, where he was to remain until his death, thirty years later. In the same year that Rennie moved to Stamford Street the Albion Mills burned down, probably as a result of arson, While the Mills pleased sightseers like Thomas Jefferson, newly appointed US Ambassador to France, they do not seem to have appealed to their own labour force.

Rennie's Stamford Street house was then numbered 27, later 52, then 18. The headquarters of his engineering business was located in nearby

Holland Street, off Blackfriars Road, where it was to remain for a century. Rennie's professional practice came to embrace canals, docks and bridges, most notably Southwark Bridge, built between 1815 and 1819. This bridge, the largest ever to be built of cast-iron, was designed with three massive spans – the centre one being 240 feet – to avoid obstructing river traffic. Praised by Robert Stephenson, it bankrupted the Rotherham firm which produced its ironwork. The bridge was sold in 1866 to the City Corporation for £218,000, a quarter of what it had cost to build. It was replaced in 1919 by the present steel structure, designed by Sir Ernest George.

In the course of working on particularly challenging coastal projects John Rennie also improved the diving-bell and devised a steam-powered bucket-chain dredger. He remained Boulton & Watt's London representative and on their behalf devised precision machinery for the Royal Mint's new establishment at Tower Hill and for Woolwich Dockyard. He also proved "friendly and welcoming to all foreign engineers who come to England to study his works and profit from his genius." Rennie's public standing was attested by a bust by Chantrey, portraits by Raeburn and Behnes and burial in St. Paul's Cathedral.

Both Rennie's engineer sons were born at his Stamford Street residence, the eldest, George (1791-1866) in the year his father moved in. George's first professional appointment was as superintendent of machinery at the Royal Mint. Although he did engineer several railway lines, George Rennie's professional interests remained with mechanical rather than civil engineering. Working mainly for the Admiralty, he built the Royal Navy's first experimental screw-propeller vessels and invented machinery for mass-manufacturing ship's biscuit. Rennie's second son, John (1794-1874) went into partnership with his elder brother on the death of their father but was destined to outshine him in the public eye, thanks largely to his reconstruction of London Bridge to his father's designs. Upon its completion in 1831 John Rennie junior was knighted, the first engineer to be so honoured since Sir Hugh Myddelton over two centuries previously for his construction of the New River. The youthful Brunel was left seething at his rival's success. Rennie, inheriting his father's position as engineer to the Admiralty, went on to do much work on improving harbours and also carried on his father's commitment to draining the Lincolnshire fens.

## LOCAL TALENTS

William Blackburn (1750-90), born in Southwark, the son of a local tradesman, was educated at the Royal Academy Schools, where he exhibited a great talent for drawing. Given his birthplace, it was perhaps appropriate that he came to specialise in designing penitentiaries and prisons and was a close friend of the pioneer of penal reform, John Howard.

John Newman (1786-1859) was a pupil of Sir Robert Smirke, architect of the British Museum. Newman's local work included extensions for the School for the Indigent Blind at St George's Fields between 1834 and 1838 (*see p56*) and St Olave's girls' school at Maze Road, built in 1839-40. Newman lived locally at Old Bridge House and became clerk to the Bridge House Trust. Although he was a founder member of the Institute of British Architects, he was, in truth, rather more interested in antiquarianism than in architecture. Newman's personal collection of antiquities included the bronze head of the emperor Hadrian now on display in the British Museum. Newman's son, A.S. Newman (1828-73), became surveyor to Guy's and to the St Olave's district board of works. Another son, A.H. Newman, succeeded to his practice.

*118.  Augustus Welby Pugin (1812-1852).*

# Writers and Poets

## JOHN GOWER

Chaucer's friend John Gower (1330-1408) lived in the priory of St Mary Overie from 1377 until his death, devoting all his time to his writing. On Gower's splendid tomb his imposing effigy rests its head on three volumes of his works – *Speculum Meditantis*, written in French, *Vox Clamantis*, written in Latin, and the *Confessio Amantis*, written in English, the latter at the direct request of Richard II, or so the author liked to claim. These various volumes thus reveal the poet to have been equally at home in the language of the court, of scholarship and of the common people. The *Speculum Meditantis*, entitled *Mirour de l'Omme* in French, is an allegory of 32,000 lines in twelve line stanzas, composed to "set forth the purposes of Providence in dealing with Man" – a work of Miltonic length and complexity to match a Miltonic mission. The apocalyptic *Vox Glamantis* of 10,000 lines includes commentary on the Peasants' Revolt of 1381, flaying the worldly churchmen and greedy lawyers who had helped to provoke rebellion. The 33,000 lines of the *Confessio Amantis* weave together, around the theme of the Seven Deadly Sins, 141 stories in octosyllabic couplets. This work appears to have had a broad European appeal because it was subsequently translated into Spanish and Portuguese. Several of the stories in the *Confessio* also appear in Chaucer's *Canterbury Tales*, which is only just over half as long, totalling some 17,000 lines in all. Gower and Chaucer, once friendly rivals, may have become estranged in later life. A tribute to Chaucer which appears in the first version of *Confessio Amantis* was removed in a later one.

Gower remarried when he was nearly seventy. His much younger bride (nurse?) was Alice Groundolf and the ceremony took place, by special permission, in the private chapel attached to his lodgings in the priory. Around 1400 Gower went totally blind. Shakespeare uses Gower as speaker of the Prologue in his *Pericles*, apparently quite confident, two centuries after the poet's death, that the groundlings would recognise his name.

## EDWARD DYER

The poet Sir Edward Dyer (1543-1607) was introduced at court by Elizabeth's favourite, Robert Dudley, earl of Leicester. Educated at Oxford, Dyer was employed as a diplomat on missions to the Netherlands in 1584 and to Denmark in 1589. He was knighted in 1596.

Dyer's surviving works amount to no more than half a dozen compositions but in his day he was highly regarded as a poet. The most famous poem associated with him, beginning, "My mind to me a kingdom is" is now thought not to have been his composition. But he did write a fine elegy on the death of his fellow poet and close friend Sir Philip Sidney. After Sidney's heroic death at the battle of Zutphen in 1586 Dyer shared out the books bequeathed to him with their mutual friend Fulke Greville. Towards the close of his life Dyer, who never married, became increasingly reclusive and retired to apartments in Winchester House, where he dabbled in chemical experiments and occasionally entertained his friend, Dr Dee, the royal astrologer. Dyer was buried in St Saviour's.

## JOHN RUSHWORTH

John Rushworth (1612-90) was trained for the law but gravitated swiftly into the maelstrom of the political crisis of the civil wars. An eyewitness of the trials of Strafford and Hampden, Rushworth was also present when Charles I memorably stormed into the Commons at the head of a column of troops in an attempt to arrest the five Members who had led the defiance to his royal authority. Rushworth's riveting transcription of the king's speech on that occasion became a canonical text for propagandists. Despite being at both Naseby and the siege of Colchester and acting as secretary to both Fairfax and Cromwell, Rushworth nevertheless successfully managed to negotiate a transition to the Restoration regime, serving as an MP and gaining several lucrative posts. Despite this and the inheritance of an estate, however, he became so deeply indebted that he spent the last six years of his life in the King's Bench prison "where, being reduced to his second childship, for his memory was quite decayed by his taking too much brandy to keep up his spirits, he quietly gave up the ghost in his lodging in a certain alley there, called Rules Court". Rushworth's eight volumes *of Historical Collections*, a compilation including both official documentation and personal accounts based on his own shorthand notes, became a prime source for early historians of the turbulent seventeenth century.

*119. Christopher Smart, 1722-1771.*

## CHRISTOPHER SMART

Christopher 'Kit' Smart (1722-71), a Cambridge-trained classical scholar, earned his living as a literary hack for the publisher John Newbery, whose stepdaughter he married. From 1757 to 1763 Smart was afflicted with a mental illness and confined but on his release returned to writing poetry and translating classical texts until poverty and debt forced him to live within the Rules of King's Bench, where he died. Smart was all but forgotten for a century and a half when the publication of his unfinished *Jubilate Agno*, composed while he was in a private asylum at Bethnal Green, confirmed his status as a highly original poet. Inspired by Hebrew verse forms, it is a hymn to the Creation, exhibiting an astonishing range of reference, from the biblical and cabalistic to the botanical and scientific.

## WILLIAM COMBE

Few but literary scholars now recognise the name of William Combe (1741-1823), despite a prolific output of over eighty works, many slight but some very weighty indeed. Combe's obscurity is the less surprising when one learns that nothing which he produced appeared in his lifetime under his name. A Bristolian by birth, he attended Eton and Oxford, but left university after little more

than a year, without taking a degree. A legacy of £2,000, topped up by an annuity of £50, from his 'godfather', a wealthy City Alderman who was almost certainly his natural parent, enabled Combe to travel to Italy, where he met Sterne. Returning to England he dabbled with the law before succumbing to the temptations of lounging around London and fashionable spas. Styling himself 'Count Combe', he looked the part well enough, being tall, handsome, elegant and witty. He kept two carriages and a retinue of servants but was soon so heavily in debt that he is said to have attempted survival as a waiter, cook, elocution teacher and common soldier before turning to authorship. His first certain work was *A Description of Patagonia* (1774), which he had, of course, never visited. In 1775 he had a play performed in Bristol but it failed to achieve print. Satirical verses became his next métier. By 1780 he was living within the Rules of King's Bench, his home for the next more than forty years. Most of his first decade there passed inconsequentially, in a literary sense, but from 1789 onwards he was reborn as a Pittite pamphleteer, a career move which brought him a modest pension whose security depended on the ebb and flow of ministries. Combe's next incarnation was as a contributor and consultant to *The Times*. The final and most fruitful phase of his life derived from his employment by the master print-maker Ackermann. The brilliant caricaturist Thomas Rowlandson supplied prints, parodying the popular travel books of the day, in celebration of the vacation peregrinations of an absurd clerical schoolmaster 'Dr Syntax'. Combe supplied the accompanying doggerel verse. They proved to be a great success, spawning a mini~series of subsequent volumes. The first title alone went through four editions in the year of its publication and by 1819 had reached its eighth edition. Combe also supplied the text to Ackermann's heavyweight histories of Westminster Abbey, Oxford and Cambridge and most of the text for a volume on the great public schools.

## MARY WOLLSTONECRAFT

Mary Wollstonecraft (1759-97) overcame a background of poverty, abuse and misfortune to achieve a brief, if controversial, literary notoriety in her own lifetime and, two centuries after her death in childbirth, acclamation as an icon of feminism. Her enthusiasm for the French Revolution inspired her *Vindication of the Rights of Women*, which called on the leaders of that

120. *Mary Wollstonecraft.*

movement to extend to all females the rights they claimed for all men. It was composed while she was living, in poverty once more, in George Street, just off Blackfriars Road. Talleyrand, among others, is said to have visited her there and taken wine out of a teacup, glasses being regarded as superfluous to her austere lifestyle. Her daughter Mary, whose birth was the cause of her own early death, was to marry the poet Shelley and write *Frankenstein*. The father of Mary Wollstonecraft's daughter was the philosopher William Godwin. Their marriage had been promoted by Mary's contemporary and friend Mary Hays (1760-1843), who shared the same circle of radical literary acquaintance, which also included William Blake, Joseph Priestley and Tom Paine. Mary Hays was born in Southwark and lived there with her mother and two unmarried sisters. Though scarcely the Haworth of the Brontes the household may also have seethed with suppressed emotions because Hays gained a notoriety of her own from auto-biographical novels of passion such as *Memoirs of Emma Courtenay* and *The Victim of Prejudice*. Hays subsequently switched to writing children's books and a six volume biographical dictionary of eminent women. She never married. Her own very belated (1993) entry in the *Dictionary of National Biography* notes mordantly "Her forth-

right depictions of female passion made her a target for satire ... Her 'exquisite misery' and longevity were ironic comment on her search for happiness and frequent wishes to be dead."

### H.F. CARY
It was while working as an obscure country cleric that H.F.Cary (1772-1844) completed his ground-breaking translation of Dante. It attracted little notice, however, until Coleridge, sauntering along the beach at Littlehampton, happened to over-hear Cary declaiming Homer in Greek to his son, introduced himself and spent the rest of the day absorbed in conversation with his new acquaint-ance. It was thanks to Coleridge's lectures (*see p64*) that Cary's work finally reached a wide public. Through Coleridge also Cary became a close friend of Charles Lamb. Cary went on to produce translations of Pindar and Aristophanes and to gain a post as a cataloguer at the British Museum. He lived in West Square when it was newly built.

### LEIGH HUNT
Leigh Hunt (1784-1859) was perhaps the most celebrated inmate of Horsemonger Lane gaol and during his sojourn there even made it something of a literary salon. The occasion of his imprison-ment was an attack in the manner of an anti-

121. *Leigh Hunt.*

encomium made on the Prince Regent in Hunt's journal *The Examiner* in 1812 to mark his target's fiftieth birthday. Hunt assailed the would-be 'First Gentleman of Europe' as "a violator of his word, a libertine over head and ears in disgrace, a despiser of domestic ties ... a man who has just closed half a century without one single claim on the gratitude of his country or the respect of posterity."

This outburst cost a sentence of two years behind bars and a fine of £500. Hunt, despite his precarious health, rejected an offer to remit both parts of his sentence in return for a pledge to refrain from further criticism of the Prince. Instead he had his cell papered to look like a trellis of roses, had the ceiling painted to look like a cloud-strewn sky and had Venetian blinds set at the windows to cut off the dismal outlook. A constant supply of fresh flowers and a constant flow of distinguished visitors, including Keats, Byron and Bentham, lifted Hunt's spirits, as did his piano and the demands of continuing to edit *The Examiner* throughout his sentence.

## THOMAS BARNES

Thomas Barnes (1785-1841) was a schoolfellow of Leigh Hunt at Christ's Hospital and followed his friend into journalism but not into literature. According to Hunt Barnes missed his vocation – "he might have made himself a name in wit and

123. *Thomas Love Peacock.*

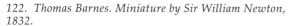

122. *Thomas Barnes. Miniature by Sir William Newton, 1832.*

literature, had he cared much for anything beyond his glass of wine and his Fielding." Whether Hunt's opinion is taken as irony or flippancy it was wide of the mark. Barnes took over editorship of *The Times* when he was just thirty-two and made it what it had never before been – a power in the land. Lord Chancellor Lyndhurst asserted that Barnes was "the most powerful man in the country". He was certainly one of the most feared; personally the soul of affability in manner and kindness in deed, but renowned for the merciless cruelty of his pen. The victims of his editorials and reviews doubtless greeted with relief Barnes' failure, while still in his journalistic prime, to return to his home in West Square following a surgical operation.

## THOMAS PEACOCK

Thomas Love Peacock (1785-1866) was the son of a London glass merchant who died when the boy was only three but left sufficient means for him to educate himself proficiently in the classical languages, French and Italian. Industrious but unfocused, Peacock initially attempted poetry, an endeavour which brought him into contact with Shelley, whose close friend he became and from whom he received an important series of letters, descriptive of the poet's experiences in Italy. Another friend was the young Henry Cole, future director of the Victoria and Albert Museum, who was to edit Peacock's works as a labour of love in his retirement. In 1816 Peacock published his satirical novel, *Headlong Hall*, following it with *Nightmare Abbey* in 1818.

In 1819 Peacock, who had shown little sustained interest in any career outside literature, was proposed for the East India Company by the company historian and passed the entrance tests with ease and the highest credit. Employment enabled Peacock to propose marriage – by letter – to Jane Gryffydh, a Welsh girl whom he had not set eyes on for eight years. Jane accepted and came to live with Peacock in Stamford Street, where his mother continued to reside with them. Rather surprisingly Peacock became an assiduous administrator, made himself an expert on steam navigation and vigorously defended the Company's interests before Parliamentary committees of inquiry. In 1856 he succeeded James Mill as Chief Examiner at the East India Company, to be succeeded in his turn by the great man's son, the philosopher John Stuart Mill. Peacock became, according to the *Dictionary of National Biography*, "a rare instance of a man improved by prosperity". His unexpected professional success was, however, offset by personal tragedy. The death of a daughter precipitated his wife into a nervous collapse and he was himself greatly grieved by the death of his mother in 1833 and the demise of the three of his four children who predeceased him.

## JOHN KEATS

Born in Moorgate, the son of an ostler, John Keats (1795-1821) initially benefited from his father's enterprising marriage to the daughter of his employer, a stable-keeper who left a fortune of £13,000. Keats showed an early passion and talent for literature but the death of his father (ironically by a fall from a horse), and then of his mother, left him at the mercy of an uncomprehending guardian who decreed that he should follow a medical career. Keats dutifully succumbed but finally broke his indentures to a surgeon of Edmonton a year early and determined to conclude his studies alone at Guy's and St Thomas's, which were then combined for

124. *John Keats, from the painting by William Hilton.*

teaching purposes. Initially lodging in Dean Street, Keats by 1815 was sharing lodgings with two other students in St Thomas's Street, above a tallow-chandler's, the precise location of which has been lost. An able enough student, Keats paid but fitful attention to his studies, such was his determination to follow his literary bent, The poet's famous sonnet *On first reading Chapman's Homer* was composed at this time. He also made the acquaintance of Leigh Hunt, then languishing in prison (*see above*); this relationship was to prove fruitful in a literary sense but in the eyes of the critics tarred Keats himself with obloquy by association as one the 'Cockney poets' snootily derided by the pundits of the *Edinburgh Review*. Despite Keats' somewhat dilatory attention to his professional studies he proved sufficiently competent to be appointed dresser (surgical assistant) to Mr Lucas at Guy's in March 1816. In July of that year he learned that he had passed with credit his Licentiate at Apothecaries' Hall. Gravitating into Leigh Hunt's circle, Keats met Shelley.

Abandoning the Borough in 1816 Keats moved to Poultry in the City, barely a few hundred yards from his birthplace. Despite having performed a number of surgical operations successfully, Keats had by now decided to abandon medicine and in 1817 published his first volume of verse, which was dedicated to Leigh Hunt.

## SHELLEY

The connection between Percy Bysshe Shelley (1792-1822) and Southwark is slight but, at least in terms of his personal life, significant. After being sent down from Oxford for gratuitously irritating bishops and college heads with a pamphlet on *The Necessity of Atheism*, Shelley went to ground in Soho, impulsively married the self-dramatising Harriet Westbrook, then dabbled in revolutionary politics and vegetarianism until the realisation dawned that his chosen life partner was more interested in millinery than the millennium. Shelley fled with the more philosophically-minded Mary Godwin (daughter of Mary Wollstonecraft) to Switzerland, taking with them Mary Jane Clairmont, the daughter of Mary Godwin's stepmother by her first marriage. This *ménage à trois* was, to say the least, open to malicious construction but that did not deter the threesome, on returning from their futile foray in search of an Alpine idyll, from taking lodgings all together at 26 Nelson Square, then but newly built, on 9 November 1814. Grievously short of cash and worried by Mary's ill-health, Shelley was rescued by an unexpected stroke of fate in the death of his grandfather. This prompted Shelley's father, a somewhat dim baronet, to settle a thousand a year on the poet, who in turn could settle £200 on the estranged Harriet and relocate himself to the more fashionable surroundings of Hans Place, Knightsbridge on 8 February 1815. It may have seemed a new beginning, though it proved but a prelude to many further trials.

125. *Percy Bysshe Shelley.*

## METHUEN

The celebrated publishing firm of Methuen was the creation of Sir Algernon Methuen Marshall Methuen (1856-1924), born Algernon Stedman in Union Street. He progressed from teaching to writing textbooks to publishing. His success was chiefly assured by his ability to spot and sign up many of the leading literary talents of his day – most notably Marie Corelli, Rudyard Kipling, Hilaire Belloc and Joseph Conrad.

# The Railway Intrudes

"There still remain some half dozen old inns, which have preserved their external features unchanged, and which have escaped alike the rage for public improvement, and the encroachments of private speculation. Great, rambling, queer, old places they are, with galleries and passages and staircases wide enough and antiquated enough to furnish material for a hundred ghost stories."

*The Posthumous Papers of the Pickwick Club*, Chapter 10.

By the time Dickens wrote this description of the Borough High Street in the winter of 1836-37 it was already an epitaph, although the process of dying was to take over half a century. The irruption of the railway was the death-knell of the famous old coaching inns, which lost their *raison d'etre* as the long distance coach succumbed to the superior speed, efficiency and cheapness of the railway. Chaucer's historic Tabard (then called Talbot) fell into disrepair, was used as storerooms, sold off in 1873 and demolished soon after. The King's Head was reincarnated as a florid gin palace in 1881. The White Hart, whose yard was the scene of the momentous first meeting between Mr Pickwick and Sam Weller, was demolished in 1889. In that same year The George, which was to be the sole survivor of this winnowing, lost its northern and central wings to make way for an extension of the railway.

In terms of the physical environment, the impact of the railway was, of course, far more devastating in the immediate area of London Bridge station itself and along the approaches to it from east and west, but that, too, happened by stages. London's first steam-powered passenger train – and the first in Britain devoted to passengers only – left Deptford on 8 February 1836 and terminated its journey at a temporary halt, Spa Road, Bermondsey. A horse bus journey of an hour was reduced to an exhilarating passage of just eight minutes. Thus was the London commuter born in south-east London, the companies building lines to the north and west of the capital being primarily interested in long-distance routes to provincial cities and regarding suburban services as a distracting nuisance.

*126. London Bridge Station, from the Illustrated London News, 15 February 1851.*

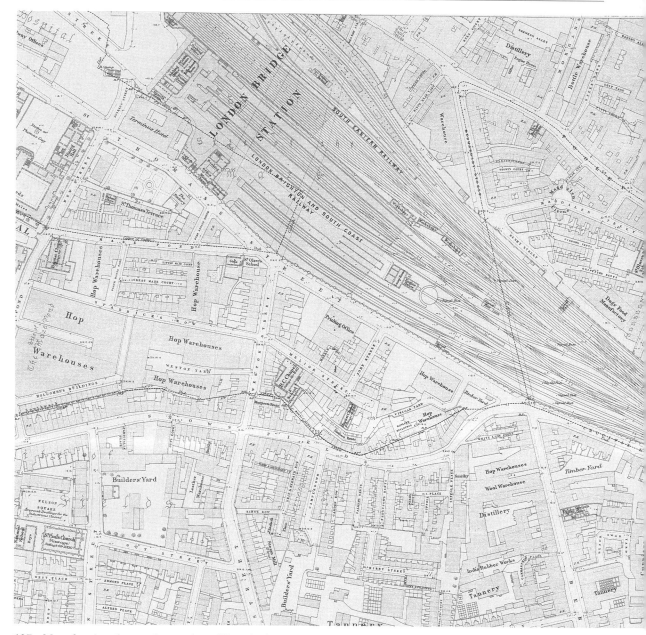

127.  *Map showing the conglomeration of lines leading to London Bridge Station, at the end of the nineteenth century.*

The four mile line was hailed as the engineering wonder of the age because it was carried on hundreds of arches, punctuated by bridges with classical columns, thus resembling a Roman aqueduct. By 1838 the line had been extended from Deptford to Greenwich. A footpath (toll one penny) ran alongside the line. Ambitious plans were mooted to build a complementary 'promenade', running parallel to the track, to enable the respectable bourgeoisie of south-east London to parade in their finery and inspect the new technological marvel as it chuffed past. It was also suggested that houses and shops might be built inside the arches. Although nothing came of these whimsies, by the end of the decade the line, boosted by day-trippers to Greenwich, was carrying two million passengers a year.

The track from Spa Road to London Bridge was completed at the end of 1836 but not until 1844 was a proper station built, in an Italianate style, to the designs of Henry Roberts (d.1876), who was actually a specialist in model dwellings for the poor. In 1849 the station was rebuilt to the designs of Samuel Beazley (1786-1851), who specialized in building theatres and also wrote over a hundred farces and comedies. Beazley's reconstruction split the station into two parts, one for the South Eastern Railway, which had taken over the original Greenwich railway, the other for the remaining companies which had amalgamated to form the London, Brighton and South Coast Railway.

Delay in providing the first proper station and the brevity of its life need occasion no surprise. Unlike the churches and schools that the Victorians built in such profusion, when it came to the railway station, there was no precedent to guide the architect. As the *Building News* confessed "The kind of termini and stations erected, when first the railway system was introduced ... is an example of our thorough inability to meet the requirements of a new class of structure. Engineers blundered ... Here and there an architect's hand was apparent." Though not, apparently, to invariable advantage. Of the exterior of London Bridge the same journal observed that it "does not display any architectural talent, though it betrays some considerable effort." The interior was "certainly bad".

The incursion of lines into the capital from all sides had prompted a Royal Commission in 1846 to call a halt to railway construction in central London. In 1860 the *Building News* warned that "the greatest danger to the health of London, to

*128. London Bridge Railway Terminus Hotel, from the Illustrated London News, 3 August 1861.*

its architectural appearance, and convenience of traffic, is to be apprehended from the penetration of railways".

Notwithstanding such strictures the ban was partially lifted to allow the authorisation of extensions at roof-top level from London Bridge as far as Charing Cross (opened 1864) and Cannon Street (1866). These projects involved large-scale demolition of housing, but no obligation on the railway companies to rehouse those they displaced. This time buildings were accommodated beneath the arches, though scarcely of the prestigious nature once so fancifully envisaged, and the daily convergence of hundreds of locomotives at a single point can only have added to local air pollution and grime. That said, the railway and the goods and passengers it transported in and out of the area, was a major sustainer, both directly and indirectly, of local employment (*see pp96-7*).

# From Dickens to the Blitz

In the early 1820s the teenage Charles Dickens lodged in Lant Street when his father was incarcerated in the Marshalsea for fourteen weeks. The Charles Dickens Primary School, opened in 1877 as Lant Street Board School, stands on the site of the author's former lodgings. Dickens described the area with sardonic affection in *Pickwick Papers*.

> There is a repose about Lant Street, in the Borough which sheds a gentle melancholy upon the soul. There are always a good many houses to let in the street; it is a by-street too and its dullness is soothing. The majority of the inhabitants either direct their energies to the letting of furnished apartments or devote themselves to the healthful and invigorating pursuit of mangling. The chief features in the still life of the street are green shutters, lodging bills, brass doorplates and bell handles, the principal specimens of animated nature the pot boy, the muffin youth and the baked potato man. The population is migratory, usually disappearing on the verge of quarterday and generally by night. Her Majesty's revenues are seldom collected in this happy valley; the rents are dubious and the water communication is very frequently cut off.

Dickens' landlord and landlady were later reincarnated as the Garlands in *The Old Curiosity Shop*.

*129. A tavern in Lant Street. Drawing by Arthur Moreland, 1931.*

*130. Lant Street. Drawing by Arthur Moreland, 1931.*

*131. Cork warehouse, Lant Street. From The Builder, 2 February 1867.*

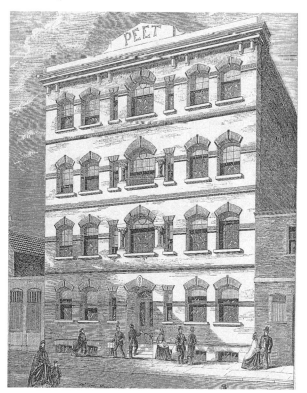

The reconstruction of London Bridge parallel to and west of its predecessor in 1830-31 (*see p110*) required a significant realignment of Borough High Street as its approach road. This involved the wholesale demolition of many buildings along its left side. The bridge itself, or rather the steps running down its western side, became a crucial location in *Oliver Twist* and henceforth became known as 'Nancy's Steps'.

## SOUTHERN SUBURBS, SOUTHWARK SQUALOR

By Dickens' time the recent construction of new bridges across the river at Vauxhall, Lambeth and Southwark had given a tremendous boost to the expansion of London's southern suburbs. In its early stages much of it clustered along major traffic arteries. Even before the advent of the new bridges Great Dover Street had been laid out in 1814 as a by-pass to the over-congested Kent (now Tabard) Street. In 1844 *The Builder* observed disparagingly how in the early years of the nineteenth century rapid ribbon development was characterised by "a kind of nondescript building, termed country box or cottage, and the roads of our suburbs were soon lined with these things of Liliputian dimensions, divided into four, six or eight cells in which people ate, drank and slept, and performed the ordinary routine of life, protecting themselves from the balmy breath of heaven by bulwarks of rheumatic-looking trees and sickly shrubs ..." Handsome houses out at Camberwell contrasted strongly with the continued deterioration of accommodation standards as one approached the Thames. Southwark's own Medical Officer of Health, the antiquary William Rendle (*see p71*), in his first ever report, composed in 1856, characterised the area gloomily as "low level and low in circumstances", the luckless victim of a trickle-down mechanism which conferred on it the detritus of the metropolis in every sense – "The lowest and poorest of the human race drop from higher and richer parishes into our courts and alleys and the liquid filth of higher places necessarily finds its way down to us. We receive the refuse as well as the outcomings of more happily situated places." Two years later Rendle observed that "Overcrowding is the normal state of our poorer districts. Small houses of four rooms are usually inhabited by three or four families and by eight, sixteen or twenty-four persons." The parish magazine of St Alphege's, Lancaster Street, endorsed his judgment, recording with distaste that "all disagreeable-smelling

*132. John Hollingshead, theatrical manager and investigative journalist (1827-1904).*

trades were carried on in the neighbourhood, haddock smokers, bone boilers, horse slaughterers." The same source estimated that more than half its adult parishioners – using that word purely in the sense of being residents in the parish – bore criminal convictions and averred that "the police come down here in companies".

Investigative journalist John Hollingshead was decidedly uncomplimentary in his description of north Southwark in *Ragged London* (1861). "A vast and melancholy property ... lighted up at intervals with special markets of industry or budding into short patches of honest trade, sinking every now and then into dark acres of crime and covered everywhere with the vilest sores of prostitution." The population of north Southwark – St Saviour's, Christ Church and St George – peaked in that same year at 89,000, ranking it, in population terms, with a fair-sized provincial city.

The expansion of Southwark's population depended on in-migration to offset the appalling environment created by overcrowding, pollution, foul water-supplies and inadequate waste-disposal services. The 1849 outbreak of cholera carried off one in twenty along Bankside, another outbreak four years later almost as many. The typhus epidemic of 1864 reached a higher mortality in the parish of St George the Martyr than anywhere else in all London. Life expectancy was and remained dismal compared to other parts of the booming capital. For the decade 1851-60 Southwark ranked sixteenth out of nineteen London districts, with a life expectancy at birth of 35.22 compared to an overall metropolitan average of 36.88. Only Stepney (17th), the City (18th) and Bermondsey (19th) ranked lower. By 1901 Southwark had improved its ranking to fourteenth (47.5 years against a metropolitan average of 49.4) but neighbouring Bermondsey had improved from nineteenth to ninth, leaving Southwark so far behind that it had become the worst district south of the river.

### FIRE!

Given the overcrowding of slum courtyards and their co-existence with foundries, rendering plants and other industrial facilities reliant on high temperature operations, fire remained an ever-present hazard. The Bankside Mustard Mills fire of 1814 caused damage estimated at £150,000. Topping's Wharf was consumed by flames in 1843, virtually destroying St Olave's church and

'Watson's Telegraph Tower'. A major fire devastated Bankside in 1855 and a far greater one swept along Tooley Street in 1861, engulfing Cotton's Wharf and Scovell's bonded warehouses, which contained a lethal mixture of saltpetre, tallow, jute, cotton and sugar. Adjoining properties held rum, paint and oil, as well as less inflammable but still readily combustible commodities such as tea and rice. Ironically Scovell's building incorporated cast-iron columns as a fire precaution but the intense heat caused by the fire taught a hitherto unsuspected and painful lesson – raised to a sufficient temperature cast-iron columns shattered when sprayed with cold water, causing whole floors to collapse in seconds.

At its height the Tooley Street conflagration stretched over three hundred yards. It burned for two days. Newspapers initially reported that damage worth £500,000 had been done. Within days this figure was dramatically revised upwards. £500,000 alone, it was calculated, would be needed just to reconstruct the buildings which had been destroyed. The value of their contents raised the damage estimate to £2,000,000.

On reflection it was concluded that the Tooley Street fire was "of an extent never equalled in the metropolis since the foundation of the Insurance

*133. Fire at Cotton's Wharf, Tooley Street, from The Illustrated London News, 29 June 1861.*

134. *James Braidwood, Superintendent of the London Fire Engine Establishment.*

Offices" – i.e. since the aftermath of the Great Fire of 1666. Nor was it to be equalled again until the Blitz of 1940-41. The insurers proposed such a massive hike in premiums that warehouse-owners and other interested parties came together to raise capital to form an entirely new enterprise to offer cover on more reasonable terms – Commercial Union, which was to thrive and grow into a major institution until it merged with Norwich Union in 2001.

Fatalities at Tooley Street were few but one was highly significant – sixty-year-old James Braidwood, commander of the Fire Brigade, killed by a falling wall and buried under its ruins. Such was his standing at the time that London firemen were often referred to as 'Jimmy Braiders'. Braidwood's terribly mutilated body was recovered two days after his death and interred with much solemnity. Contemporaries reckoned it was the largest London funeral since the Duke of Wellington's in 1852.

In 1878 the London Fire Brigade established its headquarters in Southwark Bridge Road. Its handsome, bearded commandant, Captain Eyre Massey Shaw, a noted womaniser famous enough

135. *Horse-drawn fire engine outside Tooley Street fire station.*

136. *Sir Eyre Massey Shaw, leader of the London Fire Brigade.*

137. *A new warehouse, Southwark Street, from The Builder, 27 January 1868.*

to be satirised in *Iolanthe*, lived in imposing Winchester House next door. Parts of the building dated back two centuries and had served previously as the workhouse for St Saviour's parish and later as a hat factory. The Fire Brigade finally moved out in 1937 and Winchester House subsequently became the London Fire Brigade Museum.

## 'IMPROVEMENTS'

The construction of Southwark Street in 1864 by the Metropolitan Board of Works involved the demolition of some four hundred houses, consigning an estimated four thousand inhabitants to homelessness. The widening of Tooley Street after the disastrous fire there in 1861 cleared other slums. But, because there was no obligation to rehouse the dispossessed these 'improvements' came at the cost of forcing their former inmates to crowd even more densely into dwellings that remained, for the moment, untouched. American writer Nathaniel Hawthorne was certainly dismayed by the Bankside he encountered in 1870

> It seems, indeed, as if the heart of London had been cleft open for the mere purpose of showing how rotten and drearily mean it had become. The shore is lined with the shabbiest, blackest and ugliest buildings that can be imagined ... with blind windows and wharves that look ruinous; insomuch that, had I known nothing more of the world's metropolis, I might have fancied that it had already experienced the downfall which I have heard commercial and financial prophets predict for it, within the century.

Decaying and overcrowded properties were punctuated by new constructions, both commercial and residential, several on imposing scale. Handsome Hibernia Chambers was constructed at the foot of London Bridge in 1850. On the other, eastern side of the bridge approach loomed the bare bulk of Humphrey's Wharf (1851). Pickford's Clink Street warehouses, built in 1864, rose five floors high, with cellars beneath. Southwark Street, simply taken as a thoroughfare, itself represented state of the art infrastructure with a branching network of sub-surface passages to duct gas, water, drainpipes and telephone wires into surrounding by-roads. Between 1864 and 1875 it was lined with large commercial buildings,

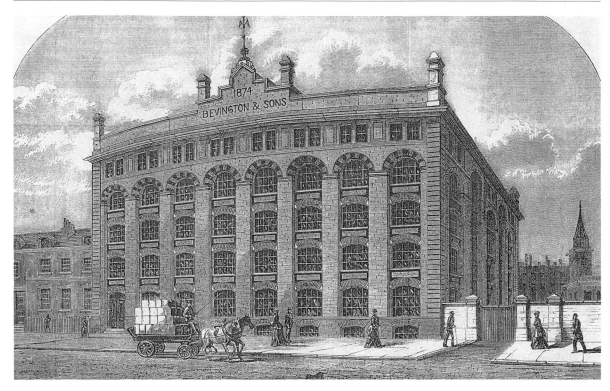

*138.  New warehouses, St Thomas's Street. From The Builder, 20 March 1875.  The architect was Henry Currey.*

most notably the imposing Hop and Malt Exchange (*see Illustration 96*), built to the designs of R.H. Moore. In 1887 the Metropolitan Board of Works initiated a programme of slum clearance in the Tabard Street area. A survey of the Park Estate in that same year, however, revealed that crammed into its fifty-eight acres were eighteen hundred dwellings, a chapel, church, school, factories, warehouses and enough metallurgical establishments to rank it as "the principal centre of the Ironfoundry trade in London." In 1893 the borough's first public baths, combining swimming pool, laundry and bathing cubicles, opened belatedly in Lavington Street.

## URBAN VILLAGE

Social investigators of the late Victorian period uncovered in Southwark a highly distinctive local community. Considering its proximity to the world's greatest international port and its own past history as an area of Flemish and Irish settlement, Southwark had acquired a remarkably homogeneous populace with strong ties to its locality. The 1881 census showed that no less than 69.8% of Southwark's inhabitants had been born in London and only 1.2% abroad. The 1901 census revealed that as the population of the newly-formed Metropolitan Borough of Southwark reached an all-time peak at 202,479, only a thousand local residents could be classified as immigrants, plus two thousand Irish – and half of them had been born in England and thought of themselves as Catholic Cockneys.

Southwark's neighbourhoods constituted an agglomeration of highly localised communities of streets and blocks and courts and alleys, a massive urban village organised around interlocking support networks of local families and the shops and markets they patronised. Public houses were crucial as arenas for socialising, sing-songs, gossip and displays of talent, dress or all too temporary wealth; they also functioned as a basis for sports teams, outings, whip-rounds and illegal betting and the place where casual or outdoor workers were paid off and work of varying degrees of honesty might often be found. Within the general populace a discernible 'Pearly' sub-culture, peculiar to the costermongers and their families also existed.

*139.  Some Southwark slums – Wagstaff Buildings, c1920.*

140.  *Vestry Hall, Walworth Road, from The Builder, 1866. This later became Southwark Town Hall.*

Romanticised at the time by music-hall super-star Albert Chevalier, and half a century later by the Lupino stage dynasty, the costers were lumped together by the would-be spiritual regenerators of St Alphege's parish with "tramps and thieves" as "blaspheming riffraff", their consorts "coarse-faced slatternly women", their all too numerous offspring "ragged, peaked-faced, hungry-eyes". Social investigators were particularly struck by the contrast between these folk, bonded to one another by ties of intermarriage, neighbourliness, friendships and feuds and the inhabitants of the new tenement blocks, a transient population of 'nomadic propensity'. There was also a striking contrast between activist Bermondsey which was both radical and overtly patriotic, and South-wark which was politically far more passive.

Charles Booth's massive 1890s *Survey of Life and Labour of the People in London* identified South-wark and Bermondsey as the only areas in the entire capital with over 50% of their local popu-lation living in poverty. Conditions were judged worst between Borough High Street and Blackfriars Road.

> It contains a number of courts and small streets which for vice, poverty and crowding, are unrivalled in London as an aggregate area of low life form perhaps the most serious blot to be reformed on the whole of our map.

The parish of St Saviour's was the poorest in all London; of 33,000 persons living between Blackfriars Bridge and London Bridge an aston-ishing 68% were classified as 'the poor'. Booth particularly noted the mechanism which rendered such poverty endemic.

> There is a deplorably low level in all parts which lie near the sources of work and this low level tends to perpetuate itself, for no sooner does anyone rise and get a bit decent than he may be expected to move out to Clapham or elsewhere.

141. *Borough Road Library, built in 1897/8 using funds donated by John Passmore Edwards. It was one of the first two public libraries in Southwark.*

142. *The Salvation Army shelter in Blackfriars Road.*

Booth also left a graphic account of the Salvation Army Shelter in Blackfriars Road, allegedly the largest in the country, accommodating between 500 and 600 of the capital's homeless each night. Half of its lodgers were regulars, working by day as newspaper-sellers, sandwich-men or bill-stickers. By charging from a penny to threepence per night the establishment managed to pay for itself and to sell tea, cocoa, bread, jam and bacon at cost. Another Salvation Army refuge, for two hundred, 'The Ark', was in Southwark Street, offering rather better accommodation and facilities for fourpence to sixpence.

## THE GREAT WAR

Poverty did not compromise patriotism. During the Great War over a hundred thousand South London men volunteered for service, many with the 24th London Regiment. From St Saviour's parish alone 344 men were to go to their deaths. In 1917 German bombing claimed the lives of three civilians working in a tea company in Southwark Street. Corporal Henry Cross of Mermaid Court was to win the Victoria Cross for recapturing two machine-guns single-handed. Leonard Keyworth, originally a Lincolnshire man, was similarly honoured. P. Lindsey Clark's arresting war memorial in Borough High Street was unveiled before huge crowds in 1924. There were also stained-glass windows honouring the local dead in both cathedrals, as well as special memorials erected by local employers such as

143.  *A homeless man on Blackfriars Bridge c.1920.*

Barclay Perkins and the local hop traders. In 1936 the Imperial War Museum, having transferred its collection from South Kensington, opened in the truncated former premises of the Bethlem Hospital.

## THE LONG GOODBYE?

Further railway intrusion and the continuing growth of industry and commerce led to another decline in the riverside population and a corresponding rise in the southern half of the borough through the out-migration of the better-off. Whereas the population of the riverside parishes tripled between 1750 and 1861 it fell by a third between 1861 and 1901. The 200,000 plus of the newly constituted Borough of Southwark in 1901 fell to 171,695 in 1931, just under what it had been in 1861. Poverty remained severe. The 1931 mean annual death rate of 13.8% was the third highest of any borough in London. At 20 acres per 1,000 inhabitants there was also a severe lack of open space.

New structures of the inter-war period included the Oxo warehouse (1928), new frontages for the Borough Polytechnic (1930) and Borough Market (1931), Dorset House (1931-3) in Southwark Street, the rebuilding of Hay's Wharf (1931) by architectural historian H.S. Goodhart-Rendel and a new warehouse for Sainsbury's, built in 1935 in Rennie Street to designs by Sir Owen Williams.

When war broke out again Southwark was bound to find itself in the front line, given that the closure of the Port of London was a major objective of Luftwaffe bombing. Some idea of the human cost can be gauged from the fact that Guy's treated over three thousand air-raid casualties in the course of hostilities in addition to carrying much of its normal burden of work. A disused section of Underground line north of Borough station eventually afforded refuge for no less than eight thousand shelterers. But nowhere was safety guaranteed. On 16 October 1940, five weeks into the Blitz, Queen's Buildings, Scovell Road suffered a direct hit; local residents in a sub-surface shelter were drowned by the outflow of a burst water-main. St Peter's Sumner Street and All Hallows, Pepper (Copperfield) Street were totally destroyed. So were Pascall's sweet factory and Jay's hat factory. Nelson Square, St George's Cathedral, Christ Church and the Rotunda were all severely damaged. The seventeenth-century terrace of timber-framed, weatherboarded 'Fishermen's Cottages' in Colombo Street survived but so badly battered that they had to be demolished anyway in 1948. Writing in 1951 Pevsner thought the Rotunda still capable of restoration but it was to be demolished in 1957-8 to make way for United Africa House.

144.  *The Albert Institution, Gravel Lane, Blackfriars Road. Founded in 1859 for the 'physical and moral well-being of the district'. It included a library, baths, washhouse and lodging rooms.*

# The Member for Southwark

Southwark was represented in Edward I's 'Model Parliament' of 1295 and was thus the first part of London outside the City proper to be recognised as worthy of representation in its own right. Its parliamentary representatives were to include Harry Bailey, celebrated host of Chaucer's Tabard Inn, the luckless Lord Mayor Bludworth who failed so signally to save London from the Great Fire of 1666 and Dr Johnson's friend and supporter, the brewer Henry Thrale (*see p94*), who was one of a sequence of brewer Members including Sir Charles Cox, John Lade, George Meggott and Edmund Halsey.

During the eighteenth and nineteenth century Southwark was served by politicians as notable for their variety as their quality.

Henry Thornton (1760-1815) was the son of a wealthy and philanthropic City merchant and followed his father's example by greatly enlarging his personal fortune and giving much of it away. Despite the deficiencies of a dismal private education and despite his principled refusal to exchange guineas for votes, Thornton was elected for Southwark when he was just twenty-two and held the seat for the rest of his life. A man of shining integrity and strong-minded independence, Thornton became a Governor of the Bank of England and one of the Commons' leading authorities on finance and taxation. A close friend of Wilberforce and a leading member of the Evangelical 'Clapham Sect', Thornton was the prime mover behind the foundation of Sierra Leone as a colony for freed slaves. As a single man Thornton gave away six-sevenths of his income. Marriage and a progeny of nine children cut this proportion back to one third, much of which went to support schools in the Borough.

Etonian George Tierney (1760-1830), like Thornton, came from a mercantile background. Eschewing the Bar for the Commons, he distinguished himself as an opponent of Pitt, to the point of a duel with pistols at Putney, from which both escaped unscathed. In 1802-4 Tierney served as treasurer to the navy under Addington and many years later briefly as Master of the Mint. He also served as titular Colonel of the Royal Southwark Volunteers. Despite his acknowledged expertise in matters of finance, despite his energy in the conduct of business and effectiveness in debate, Tierney was hampered among the Whigs by his commercial origins and overshadowed by the indolent brilliance of Fox – altogether a 'nearly man'.

The performance of Parliamentary duties doubtless came as a relatively gentle coda to the dramatic career of General Sir Robert Wilson (1777-1849). At the age of seventeen Wilson had fought three battles in a single week, so distinguishing himself that within a month he was entrusted with command of a rearguard action. He later fought in Egypt, South Africa, Portugal and eastern Europe and was decorated by the governments of Turkey, Russia, Prussia, Austria and Portugal. A general at thirty-six, an early opponent of flogging and a prolific author on military affairs, Wilson was chosen by the electors of Southwark in 1818, 1820, 1826 and 1830. Despite voting for the reform of the franchise, Wilson left the Commons in 1831, fearing that republicanism was just around the corner. He later served as governor of Gibraltar and was buried in Westminster Abbey, leaving a family of thirteen children.

As a youth Sir William Molesworth (1810-55) combined delicate health with a sufficiently spirited temper to go all the way to Germany to fight an inconclusive duel with his former Cambridge tutor. Elected to the reformed Commons at twenty-two, he become an acolyte of the banker-historian George Grote, a friend of John Stuart Mill and his father and a specialist on colonial policy, campaigning against transportation and for colonial self-government. A founder member of the Reform Club and editor of the works of the philosopher Thomas Hobbes, Molesworth became MP for Southwark in 1845 and held the seat until his death. He attained Cabinet rank as first commissioner of the Board of Works and was personally responsible for opening Kew Gardens to the public on Sundays.

Molesworth was briefly succeeded by Admiral Sir Charles Napier (1786-1860), whose colourful and enthusiastically self-promoted career as a commerce raider, promoter of steam navigation, commander of the Portuguese fleet and captor of the port of Acre, had netted him British and Portuguese honours, a diamond-hilted sword and the freedom of the City of London. By the time he became MP for Southwark, however, the swarthy hero of Napoleonic days had become a

145. *Counting votes at a Southwark election, from the* Illustrated London News, *10 July 1852.*

stout, slovenly, slouching, stooping, snuff-stained absentee, obsessed with growing turnips on his Hampshire estate and conducting a lengthy vendetta by correspondence with the Board of Admiralty.

Napier was succeeded by A.H. Layard (1817-94), renowned to later generations as the pioneering excavator of Nimrud and Nineveh. Layard had come to archaeology more or less by accident, having wangled himself a semi-official position as a British spy in the domains of the Ottoman Sultan. His real passions, however, were politics and paintings. While MP for Southwark Layard served as under-secretary for foreign affairs and chief commissioner of works, resigning the latter post and his seat in 1868 to become ambassador in Madrid. Most of his later life was passed in Italy, writing about art.

Thorold Rogers (1823-90) is known to generations of economic historians as the pioneering student of the history of agriculture and prices in England. Ex-cleric, ex-classicist and first professor of economics at King's College, London Rogers was also a doughty controversialist and supporter of progressive causes such as elemen-

tary education and the co-operative movement. His public stance cost him a chair at conservative Oxford but won him the support of the electors of Southwark, whom he represented from 1880 to 1885. Rogers' co-member was Arthur Cohen QC (1829-1914), Britain's leading expert on shipping law. Cohen had been the first professing Jew to graduate from Cambridge, where he had also been President of the Union. He epitomised the Victorian gentlemanly ideal in courtesy, dignity, integrity and intellect, eventually serving as President of the Board of Deputies and chairman of the Bar Council.

George Isaacs (1883-1979) came of three generations of printers. At twenty-six he had become General Secretary of the National Society of Operative Printers and Assistants, a post he was to hold for forty years. Isaacs served as mayor of Southwark in 1919-21 and as its MP in 1929-31 and from 1939 to 1959. In 1945 he became chairman of the TUC and as Minister of Labour in Attlee's government administered the demobilisation of five million men from the armed forces.

# Rediscovering Hope

Bankside has now become a favoured habitat of one of the most distinctive breeds of Londoner – the famous 'Blue Badge' tourist guide. Any day of the week will find them shepherding groups in and out of Tate Modern in the old Bankside power station, or the Globe ("Listen, please. Back here. One o'clock OK, everybody?"), indicating a fine view of St Paul's from the perspective of the Millennium Bridge, suggesting that Yes, indeed, Southwark Cathedral is well worth a look inside or confirming that *HMS Belfast* is not just visiting. Half a century ago all this would have been inconceivable.

Blue Badge guides originated as the Guild of Guide Lecturers, founded in 1950 to provide a truly professional guiding service for the hordes of visitors anticipated for the forthcoming Festival of Britain. The Festival, a century on from the Great Exhibition of 1851, was meant to be "a tonic for the nation" after years of wartime rationing and also an advertisement to the world that Britain was back in business. Wags observed that in fact Britain was like the rocket-shaped Skylon which seemed to float in mid-air, dominating the Festival site in the shadow of County Hall – "without visible means of support".

The Festival of Britain was the brainchild of Herbert Morrison, whose grandson Peter Mandelson was to have an altogether less happy experience with the Millennium Dome half a century later. Morrison, a civic patriot to the core – his ashes were scattered on the Thames – was a South Londoner by birth and chose as his title Baron Morrison of Lambeth. But even his pride and loyalty would surely have been in conflict with his credulity if he had overheard one of those fledgling Blue Badge guides suggest that, having marvelled at the Dome of Discovery, visitors should next head eastwards, along the river to explore the rich heritage of Bankside and the Borough. Even the *Survey of London* volume on Bankside, published in 1950, while emphasising the immense historical importance of the area, conceded that it had become a wilderness of warehouses, gloomy, noisy and often noisome as well. *Here's England*, a 1951 guide-book for American tourists, which devoted over half its pages to London, recommending over a hundred 'must see' sites and sights, mentioned just two south of the river – the Imperial War Museum ("War relics of all kinds") and Southwark Cathedral ("where the founder of Harvard College is said to have been baptized"). Most guide books of that decade simply ignored the area, a few actually discouraged visiting it.

In the 1950s the Upper Pool, between London and Tower Bridges, was still operating at peak capacity in handling cargoes of commodities. Within twenty years all that would vanish, a

146. *Destined for demolition – Nelson Square, off Union Street, 1951.*

casualty of the shipping revolution represented by containerisation and bulk-carriers. As cargo-handling and its associated storage and distribution functions disappeared so did linked processing activities and manufacturing. The relentlessness and scale of these trends may not have been easy to perceive at the time. The opening of a major press for Her Majesty's Stationery Office in Pocock Street in 1961 and of Bankside power station in 1963 may well seem to have reaffirmed the essentially industrial character of the area.

In the larger context of London's transformation from a great port city, dealing in physical commodities, to a centre of global tourism, dealing in images and experiences, it may seem inevitable that riverside Southwark should also be transformed. Even more compelling than the intrinsic depth of its historic heritage was its simple proximity to the City. New needs were emerging in the tourism market. Repeat visitors would no longer be content to 'do' the Tower and the Abbey yet again and the 'honeypot sites', in any case, were fast reaching saturation point. Many London districts were, however, slow to

capitalise on their 'visitor potential'. In this respect the newly-formed London Borough of Southwark was no worse than most. But its torpor was compounded by an attitude to the local economy which was fundamentally backward-looking, striving to retain or recapture the sort of 'real' trades whose employees had for so long provided its electoral base.

The catalysts of change were to come from outside and largely innocent of any wider purpose in terms of the economic regeneration of the area as a whole. When Sam Wanamaker established the Globe Playhouse Trust in 1970 he did so because Bankside was where the Globe once stood. When *HMS Belfast* moored at Hay's Wharf and opened as a visitor attraction in 1971 it did so because that was as near to its institutional parent, the Imperial War Museum, as it could conveniently be located. The hop trade folded up the following year, bacon curing, brewing and power generation ended within the next decade. The first few portents of an impending employment renaissance based on visitor spending began to appear piecemeal rather than as the realisation

*147.  The new Globe Theatre.*

148.  *The Bankside Power Station now transformed into the Tate Modern – a success story that has brought many new visitors to Southwark.*

149.  *The Millennium Bridge, opened for a brief time in 2000, was to provide a direct walkway from St Paul's to Southwark and, in particular, to the Tate Modern and the Globe.  Unfortunately it was found to move alarmingly when there were too many people on the bridge and work has since continued to remedy this.  At the time of writing (August 2001) it is still not open to the public.*

150. *The former Oxo warehouse, just to the west of Blackfriars Bridge, was built in 1928. It is surmounted by a tower 202 feet high, then the second highest building in London. As advertising on such high buildings was not permitted Oxo had their name contrived out of the windows in the tower which was lit up at night. The building is now used for apartments and community groups, together with a restaurant that has magnificent river views.*

of a considered strategy. The Bankside Gallery opened in 1980. Nearby the Founders' Arms was designed in a contemporary mode, with extensive outdoor seating provided in the expectation, or at least hope, that patrons might be expected to linger and enjoy one of the finest sunset views that the capital can afford. The ancient Anchor followed the same cue. Hay's Galleria opened in 1988, holding out the pleasing prospect of a continuous riverside walkway. Since the opening of the Globe in 1993 the pace has only quickened. From Blackfriars Bridge to the Design Museum sufficient attractions have come into existence to achieve that critical mass which is required to make a visitor feel it would be well worthwhile to spend an entire day 'south of the river'. For

the ghoulish there are the rival attractions of the Clink Prison, the London Dungeon and the Old Operating Theatre, for the gourmet the Borough Market, Vinopolis, the Tea and Coffee Museum and over a hundred places to eat and drink, offering not only predictable Indian and Italian cuisine but Turkish and even Peruvian as well.

In its first year Tate Modern topped its most optimistic visitor target by a factor of three. The opening of the Jubilee Line and the Millennium Bridge (albeit spoiled by constructional problems) exemplified and symbolised the reconnection of the area with the rest of the metropolis. It was altogether fitting that the first year of the new millennium should be marked by the rediscovery of the site of a theatre called Hope.

# Chronology

1066  William I devastates Southwark.
1096  First mention of St Olave's Church.
1106  Augustinians take St Mary Overie.
1122  First mention of the church of St George the Martyr.
1162  Regulations issued for the Bankside stews.
1163-9  London Bridge rebuilt.
1176-1209  London Bridge built in stone.
1212  Fire devastates St Mary Overie.
1213  Re-establishment of St Thomas's Hospital.
1218-19  Causeway built on Bankside.
1276  London Bridge Market suppressed.
1306  First mention of the Tabard Inn.
1309-10  Frost Fair on the Thames.
1327  City of London acquires limited control over Southwark.
1381  June 13 Wat Tyler & John Ball reach Southwark during Peasants' Revolt.
1384-6  London Bridge chapel rebuilt.
1437  London Bridge Gatehouse collapses.
1446  Rosary acquired by Sir John Fastolf.
1450  2nd July Jack Cade occupies Southwark.
1462  Southwark Fair chartered.
1469  Nave roof of St Mary Overie collapses.
1504  Mass break-out from the Marshalsea prison.
1506  Bankside stews suppressed for a year.
1536  New burial ground opened for St Margaret's Church.
1539  St Margaret and St Mary Magdalene united as St Saviour's.
1546  Bankside stews closed.
1550  Southwark becomes Bridge Ward Without.
1551  St Thomas's Hospital re-founded.
1555  Trial of Protestant martyrs at the Consistory Court in St Saviour's.
1562  St Saviour's Grammar School established.
1571  St Olave's Grammar School established.
1577  Nonesuch House built on London Bridge.
1584  Cure's College Almshouses established in Deadman's Place.
1587  Rose Theatre built.
1592, 1593  Apprentices riot against alleged loss of jobs to foreigners.
1595  Swan Theatre built.
1599  Globe Theatre built.
1602  First production of *Hamlet* at the Globe; riot at the Swan.
1607-8  Frost Fair on the Thames.
1613  Globe Theatre burned down.
1614  Hope Theatre built.
1618  Southwark pottery established.

1621  Frost Fair on the Thames.
1625  Epidemic of plague.
1629  Tabard Inn rebuilt.
1633  Fire on London Bridge.
1634-7  Outbreaks of plague.
1639  Riot at the Marshalsea prison.
1642  Winchester House becomes a prison for Royalists.
      Bankside theatres suppressed.
1644  Globe Theatre demolished.
1651  Hay's Wharf established.
1658  Newcourt's map of Borough and Bankside.
1671  Parish of Christ Church established.
1675  Riots against weaving machines.
1676  Fire from oil shop devastates northern Southwark.
1677  Frost Fair on the Thames.
1681  St Saviour's parish school opened.
1682  Last bear-pit closed on Bankside.
1683-4  Frost Fair on the Thames.
1686  Borough Town Hall built.
1689  Fire devastates Borough High Street.
1698  St George the Martyr parish school opened.
1702-3  St Thomas's Church built.
1703  Dr Richard Mead appointed to St Thomas's Hospital.
1706  Rebuilding work at St Thomas's.
1715-16  Frost Fair on the Thames.
1721  Guy's Hospital established.
      Doggett's Coat and Badge Race established.
1722  'Keep Left' rule introduced on London Bridge.
1723  Abolition of Southwark Mint as safe area.
1725  Guy's Hospital opened.
1726  Fire on London Bridge.
1730  Dog and Duck Spa opens in St George's Fields.
1732  Hopton's Almshouses established.
1733  Parish of St John Horselydown established.
1734  Thomas Guy's statue erected.
1736  Church of St George the Martyr opened.
1737-40  St Olave's Church, Tooley Street, rebuilt to the designs of Henry Flitcroft.
1738  Christ Church rebuilt.
1739-40  Frost Fair on the Thames.
1742  Southwark hatters beat an unapprenticed labourer to death.
1751  Borough Road opened.
1755-6  Site of Borough market moved to The Triangle.
1757  Houses demolished on London Bridge.
1758  Temporary London Bridge burned.
1761  Bear tavern demolished.
1762-3  Southwark Fair suppressed.

**1769** Blackfriars Bridge opened.

**1769-71** Robert Mylne lays out St George's Fields.

**1771** (Alice) Overman's Almshouses established. Obelisk erected at St George's Circus.

**1772** Magdalen Hospital moves from Whitechapel to Southwark.

**1773** St George's Fields windmill demolished.

**1780** Gordon rioters assemble at St George's Fields.

**1781** Robert Barclay buys Thrale's Anchor Brewery
Union Street laid out.

**1782** Royal Circus and Equestrian Philharmonic Academy opens at 124 Blackfriars Road.

**1783** Surrey Chapel opened.

**1787** Union Street (Methodist) Independent Chapel established.

**1790** Potts' Vinegar Manufactory moves to Southwark.

**1791** Rennie's engineering works established. Building of West Square begins.

**1793** Southwark Town Hall and Court House pulled down and rebuilt.
Philanthropic Society moves to St George's Fields.

**1798** Joseph Lancaster established his first school in Borough Road.

**1801** population 62,669.

**1801-22** Grand Surrey Canal built.

**1800-2** School for Indigent Blind established at site of the Dog and Duck.

**1806** British and Foreign Schools Society established.
Welsh congregation established in Little Guildford Street

**1807-14** Nelson Square built.

**1814** Remains of Winchester Palace revealed by fire.
Great Dover Street laid out.
Bankside gasworks opened.

**1815** Bethlem Hospital moves to St George's Fields

**1819** Southwark Bridge opened.
Blackfriars Type Foundry opens in Blackfriars Road.

**1820** Drapers' almshouses rebuilt.

**1824-31** Southwark Bridge built by Rennie.

**1828** Phoenix gasworks opened.

**1829** Great Surrey Street renamed Blackfriars Road.

**1830** Chapel of St Saviour's demolished for road widening.
King Edward's School moves to St George's Fields.

**1831** Rennie's London Bridge opened.
Thomas Cure's almshouses rebuilt.

**1834** Bankside waterworks closed.

**1836** London Bridge Station opened.

**1838** Baptist Surrey Tabernacle built in Borough Road.

**1839** General Baptist Chapel built in Borough Road.

**1841** Royal South London Dispensary established.

**1841-8** St George's Cathedral built.

**1842** Marshalsea prison closed.

**1846** Parish of St Peter, Sumner Street established.

**1849** London Bridge Station rebuilt.
Major cholera epidemic.

**1850** Parish of St Jude, St George's Road established.

**1853** St Olave's burial ground closed.
Major cholera outbreak.

**1855** Major fire on Bankside.

**1855-6** Hay's Dock built by William Cubitt.

**1857** South London Ophthalmic Hospital established at St George's Circus.

**1858** Parish of St Paul, Westminster Bridge Road established.

**1859** Southwark Town Hall demolished.

**1861** Tooley Street fire.
Terminus Hotel rebuilt at London Bridge station.

**1863-4** Borough Market buildings by Habershon, Jarvis and Jarvis.

**1864** Southwark Street built by Metropolitan Board of Works.
Tooley Street and Jamaica Road widened.
Pickford's Wharf warehouse built in Clink Street.
Cromwell Flats built.
Typhus outbreak.

**1866** Southwark Bridge sold to City Corporation for £218,000.
London Bridge-Cannon Street line opened.

**1867** Hop and Malt Exchange opened.
Charlotte Sharman opens an orphanage in West Square.

**1869** Sainsbury's moves to Southwark.
Rebuilt Blackfriars Bridge opened by Queen Victoria.
Evelina Hospital established.

**1871** Parish of St Alphege established.

**1872** Peabody Square built.

**1872-3** Borough Welsh Congregational Chapel built off Southwark Bridge Road.

**1874** Bevington's warehouse built at 42 Tooley Street.

**1875** Talbot Inn demolished.
Albert Institute demolished.
South Metropolitan Temperance Hall built.

**1875-84** Charlotte Sharman orphanage built in Austral (then South) Street.

**1876** Surrey Chapel taken over by Primitive Methodists.
Parish of All Hallows, Copperfield Street established.
**1878** Central Fire Brigade station opened in Southwark Bridge Road.
**1879-80** All Hallow's, Copperfield Road built to the designs of Sir George Gilbert Scott.
**1879** St Jude's Church built in St George's Road.
**1880** South Metropolitan Gas Company established.
**1880-2** St Alphege's, Lancaster Street built.
**1881** King's Head built.
Parish of St Michael and All Angels, Lant Street established 1884.
Charterhouse Mission established in Tabard Street.
**1887** Redcross Hall and Cottages built.
Metropolitan Board of Works clears slums in the Tabard Street area.
**1888** Marshalsea Road built.
**1889** Morley College opened.
White Hart Inn demolished.
Guy's Dental School established.
**1890** Sainsbury's depot opens at Running Horses Yard, Blackfriars Road.
King's Arms built.
Borough Underground Station opened.
**1890-2** Royal London Ophthalmic Hospital built.
**1891** Roman Catholic Church of the Most Precious Blood established.
Women's University Settlement established in Nelson Square.
Bankside power station opens.
**1893** Terminus Hotel converted to offices.
Public baths opens in Lavington Street.
**1898** St Hugh's Church, Charterhouse Mission dedicated.
Public libraries opened in Borough Road and Blackfriars Road.
**1900** Metropolitan Borough of Southwark established by the amalgamation of the civil parishes of St Saviour's, St George's, Christ Church and St Mary Newington.
**1901** Population of Metropolitan Borough of Southwark 202,479.
**1903** New St Saviour and St Olave's School buildings opened.
**1905** St Saviour's designated Cathedral of diocese of Southwark.
**1907** Harvard Chapel dedicated in Southwark Cathedral.
**1910** Blackfriars Bridge widened.

**1913** Sainsbury's opens new headquarters building, Stamford House.
**1917** Southwark Street bombed.
**1919** Southwark Bridge demolished and rebuilt.
**1920** The Hop and Malt Exchange suffers major damage from fire.
**1921** South Bridge rebuilt.
**1922** London School of Printing moves to Stamford Street.
**1924** St Saviour's parish war memorial in Borough High Street unveiled.
**1926** St Olave's, Tooley Street demolished.
**1927** Official licensing of street trades by boroughs.
**1928** Demolition of St Olave's, Tooley Street completed.
Oxo Tower built.
**1930** Bethlem Hospital moves to Beckenham.
**1931** Hay's Wharf rebuilt.
New entrance for Borough Market built.
**1931-2** Sumner Buildings, Sumner Street built.
**1934** Surrey Theatre closes.
**1935** Stopher House, Silex Street built.
**1936** Imperial War Museum opened in former Bethlem Hospital.
Geraldine Mary Harmsworth Park opened.
**1937** The George becomes a National Trust property.
**1938** South Metropolitan Gas Company moves to Beckton.
**1939** Pakeman House, Pocock Street built.
**1940** Bombing destroys the Ring, shelters at Ewer Street and Keyworth Street.
**1944** V-1 kills over fifty people in Union Street.
**1956-7** St Thomas's Operating Theatre rediscovered.
**1958** Leverian Museum (Rotunda) demolished.
Rebuilding of St George's Cathedral completed.
Remains of a Roman boat discovered at Guy's.
**1959** St Christopher House, Southwark Street built.
**1961** New Guy's House opens.
HMSO press opens in Pocock Street.
**1963** New Bankside power station opens.
**1965** The Metropolitan Boroughs of Bermondsey, Camberwell and Southwark merge to form the London Borough of Southwark.
**1967** South London Industrial Mission established at Christ Church.
**1970** Sam Wanamaker establishes the Globe Playhouse Trust.
Elizabeth Newcomen School closes.
South Bank Polytechnic formed by merger.
**1971** *HMS Belfast* opens as a visitor attraction.
Tooley Street warehouse fire.

1972  Bear Gardens Museum and Arts Centre founded.
   Southwark hop trade closes down.
1973  Rebuilt London Bridge opens.
1975  Guy's Tower opened; accommodates relocated Evelina Hospital.
1977  John Harvard Library opens.
   Roman well and sculptures discovered beneath the crypt of Southwark Cathedral.
1978  Scovell estate built.
1980  Southwark Bacon Drying Company closes.
   Bankside Gallery opened.
1981  Brandon House built.
   Market Brewery established.
   Bankside power station ceases generation.
1982  Closure of Courage's Park Street brewery.
1987  Site of The Rosary discovered.
1988  Hay's Galleria opens.
   Site of Rose Theatre rediscovered.
   The Queen opens Southwark Cathedral Chapter House.
1989  Ludgate House built.

1992  South Bank Polytechnic assumes University status.
1993  Globe Theatre opens.
1994  Globe Education Centre opens.
1995  Conversion of Bankside power station begins.
1995-6  Excavation of the site of Benbow House.
1996  *Golden Hinde* berthed at St Mary Overie's Dock.
   Obelisk returned to St George's Circus.
1998  Peace Park opened in Geraldine Mary Harmsworth Park by the Dalai Lama.
   Jerwood Foundation opens in Union Street.
2000  Tate Modern opened.
   Jubilee Line extension opened.
2001  Site of the Hope Theatre rediscovered.
   Nelson Mandela opens Southwark Cathedral Library, restaurant and Exhibition Centre.

# Further Reading

Archaeology in Southwark: *The results of archaeological investigations in the London Borough of Southwark 1998-99* (London Borough of Southwark 1999).

J.M. Beattie: *Crime and the Courts in England 1660-1800* (OUP 1986).

Mrs E. Boger: *Bygone Southwark* (Simpkin, Marshall 1895).

Jeremy Boulton: *Neighbourhood and Society: A London Suburb in the Seventeenth Century* (Cambridge University Press 1987).

Robert W. Bowers: *Sketches of Southwark Old and New* (William Wesley & Son 1905).

Martha Carlin: *Medieval Southwark* (The Hambledon Press 1996).

M. Concanen and A. Morgan: *The History and Antiquities of the Parish of St Saviour's, Southwark* (1795).

Carrie Cowan: *Below Southwark: the archaeological story* (London Borough of Southwark 2000).

James Drummond-Murray, Chris Thomas and Jane Sidell: *The Big Dig: Archaeology and the Jubilee Line Extension* (Museum of London Archaeology Service 1998).

Grace Golden: *Old Bankside* (Williams and Norgate (1951).

Charles Graves: *The Story of St Thomas's 1106-1947* (Faber & Faber 1947).

Florence Higham: *Southwark Story* (Hodder and Stoughton 1955).

Stephen Humphrey: *Southwark: The Twentieth Century* (Sutton Publishing 1999).

Stephen Humphrey: *Southwark in Archives* (London Borough of Southwark 2000).

David J. Johnson: *Southwark and the City* (OUP 1969)

Peter Marcan: *Visions of Southwark* (Peter Marcan Publications 1997).

W.J. Meymott: *An Historical Account of the Parish of Christ Church, Surrey* (1881).

Horace Monroe: *The Story of Southwark Cathedral* (Raphael Tuck 1935).

Leonard Reilly: *Southwark: An Illustrated History* (London Borough of Southwark 1998).

Leonard Reilly and Geoff Marshall: *The Story of Bankside* (London Borough of Southwark 2001).

*Survey of London*: Vol. XXII Bankside (LCC 1950).

*Survey of London*: Vol. XXV St George's Fields (LCC 1955).

Charles White: *The Metropolitan Borough of Southwark Official Guide* (Ed. J. Burrow & Co.).

R.W. Wingent: *Historical Notes on The Borough and the Borough Hospitals* (Ash & Co. 1913).

# INDEX
## Asterisks denote illustrations or captions